"Where Did We Go Wrong?"

For several decades parents have been taught that the environment of a child is crucial to his growth and development. And indeed it is. However, there is more to what makes a child tick than the influence of his parents and the home in which he grows up, as important as those are. And parents have little or no control over some of those other factors.

How then can they be held responsible for all of what a child becomes? Why should society blame parents for more than their fair share?

Sometimes, though, we parents are quick to blame ourselves when our children step out of line. We hurry to pack our bags for a guilt trip.

From the first chapter,
PARENTING WITHOUT GUILT

*****

"An insightful book . . . needed centuries ago . . . not only would I encourage every parent to invest time in the pages of this resource, but I would also encourage prospective parents to experience this journey before their first-born invades their lives."

From the foreword by
H. Norman Wright

Parenting Without Guilt

Marilyn McGinnis

Here's Life Publishers

Published by
HERE'S LIFE PUBLISHERS, INC.
P. O. Box 1576
San Bernardino, CA 92402

HLP Product No. 951707
©1987, Marilyn McGinnis
All rights reserved.

Printed in the United States of America.

Library of Congress Cataloging-in-Publication Data
McGinnis, Marilyn.
  Parenting without guilt.
  Includes bibliographies.
  1.Parents — Attitudes. 2. Guilt. 3. Parent and child.
4. Child psychology. I. Title.
HQ755.83.M37 1987   649'.1   86-33656
ISBN 0-89840-179-8 (pbk.)

Scripture quotations marked KJV are from the Authorized or King James Version of the Bible. Those marked NIV are from the Holy Bible, New International Version, ©1973, 1978, International Bible Society. Quotations marked RSV are from the Revised Standard Version of the Bible, copyrighted 1946, 1952, ©1971, 1973 by the Division of Christian Education of the National Council of Churches of Christ in the U.S.A. Quotations marked TLB are from The Living Bible, ©1971 by Tyndale House Publishers, Wheaton, Illinois. Those marked NEB are from the New English Bible, ©Oxford University Press, 1961, 1970. Other quotations are from the Berkeley Translation.

FOR MORE INFORMATION, WRITE:

L.I.F.E. — P.O. Box A399, Sydney South 2000, Australia
Campus Crusade for Christ of Canada — Box 300, Vancouver, B.C., V6C 2X3, Canada
Campus Crusade for Christ — Pearl Assurance House, 4 Temple Row, Birmingham, B2 5HG, England
Campus Crusade for Christ — P.O. Box 240, Colombo Court Post Office, Singapore 9117
Lay Institute for Evangelism — P.O. Box 8786, Auckland 3, New Zealand
Great Commission Movement of Nigeria — P.O. Box 500, Jos, Plateau State Nigeria, West Africa
Campus Crusade for Christ International — Arrowhead Springs, San Bernardino, CA 92414, U.S.A.

*To
Ron Widman
who gave me my start in writing
and to whom
my thanks is long overdue*

Contents

Foreword	9
Preface	11
1. The Guilt Trip	15
2. Why Guilt Is a Problem Today	23
3. The Power of Perception	35
4. Whatever Happened to Sin?	45
5. Free to Choose	57
6. Confronting the Ghosts of the Past	67
7. Countering Negative Thoughts	77
8. Coping With Your Accusers	91
9. Learning to Let Go of Your Children	101
10. Learning to Let Go of Guilt	115
Notes	125

Foreword

Guilt and parenting — they seem to go hand in hand for some parents. We have an abundance of advice and child-rearing methods to assist us in this journey and we look for the guaranteed approach. Marilyn McGinnis has dared to tackle the topic and has created an insightful book which was needed centuries ago — *Parenting Without Guilt*. Parents tend to feel guilt for reasons ranging from attempting to meet excessively high expectations to feeling that they alone are responsible for the behavior of their children.

In this well-constructed and readable book, the author evidences her own extensive thought on the subject as well as her extensive research. It is a resource that presents not only helpful facts and background material but also practical steps to deal with our feelings as parents. It is a how-to book written to assist us in understanding the child as well as in understanding our own feelings. Most parents face two important tasks: learning to evaluate their parental role realistically and learning to relinquish their children. This book will help parents accomplish both of these goals.

Not only would I encourage every parent to invest time in the pages of this resource, but I would also encourage prospective parents to experience this journey before their first-born invades their lives.

H. Norman Wright
Professor, Therapist, Author

Preface

The scenarios go something like this:

SCENE 1

"Jennifer," you say firmly to your fifteen-year-old, "If you don't clean up your room, and I do mean clean, by five o'clock tonight, you're not going to the party."

"Maw — um!" Her pitiful wail follows you down the hall and into the family room. Only a child can turn a one-syllable word like Mom or Dad into two.

And with that one-word opening line, the barrage of guilt-producing statements begins.

"I *did* clean my room. Can't you tell?" (Of course not! Mother is not too bright because anyone who does not first fall over the shoes in Jennifer's doorway can see that the room is clean.)

You remind Jennifer of the rug burn on your knees which occurred when you tripped over her shoes, and you say once again, "You must clean up your room."

"The room is as clean as I want it. I like it that way." (Mom is a perfectionist who delights in making unreasonable demands of her daughter. Shame on you, Mom, for not allowing your daughter to express herself in her own way.)

At 5:15, when you discover that Jennifer still has not cleaned her room, you inform her — amidst her shouts and screams of unfairness — that she will not be attending the party and that's that. Jennifer returns to her partially cleaned room to sulk for the rest of the night. You go about the evening chores feeling angry and guilty. Why guilty? Because Jennifer is unhappy — and you are the one who made her that way.

Or are you?

SCENE 2

The day your ten-year-old son comes home from the barber shop with a new haircut is the day Aunt Tillie comes to call — *dear* Aunt Tillie.

"I see Thomas has a short haircut," she says crisply. "I believe you call it a buzz" (a.k.a. crew cut, flat top, whatever). Her gaze is cutting, emphatic. "The only time a young man should have hair that short is when he enters the military. The poor child is only ten." (You are a pushy parent who is forcing your child to grow up too soon.)

SCENE 3

You get caught in traffic and are forty-five minutes late picking up your child at day-care. The attendants are understanding but you leave with your child in hand and your stomach in knots. You're frustrated at the pile of work you left behind and angry at the other drivers who made you late. But the primary gnawing inside is one of guilt — for not being able to manage your hours and get your work done in order to pick up your child on time. Your child is excited to see you, but your guilt leaves you distracted and unable to give him your undivided attention.

*****

So often, guilt starts as soon as your first child is born.

You feel guilty because you're so tired you can't keep your eyes open and your new baby just has to be fed.

You feel guilty because sometimes your adorable little toddler drives you wacko.

You feel guilty when you want some time to yourself away from the kids.

Mothers feel guilty if they work outside the home — and they feel guilty if they don't.

Two fathers have told me they feel guilty when they

yell at their kids. One was taught never to yell at kids — the other remembers his mother always yelling and he doesn't want to be like her.

There are two types of guilt: *true guilt* that results from breaking a moral law, and *false guilt* that comes from assuming we have done wrong when in reality we have not. True guilt, if we are willing to acknowledge it, can lead to forgiveness, reconciliation and growth. False guilt, on the other hand, is destructive. It robs us of peace and joy and contentment. False guilt can never be forgiven — it can only be eliminated. Neither God nor another person can forgive you when you have done nothing wrong.

My purpose in this book is to help you (1) to define more precisely your role as parent — what you are responsible for in bringing up your children and what you are not responsible for — and (2) to identify and get rid of the false guilt that robs you of the joy of parenting.

Before you begin chapter 1, however, take a few minutes to do the Agree or Disagree? checklist on page 14. Ask your mate to do the same and discuss your answers. Some of the statements are deliberately tricky to make you *think* and *question*. When you finish reading the book, look back at your answers and see if you would change any of them.

A special word of thanks to Nathan Burow for his contributions to chapter 3, and to his wife Edna for carefully evaluating the entire manuscript. Norm Wright has helped me see the manuscript through to completion and I deeply appreciate his foreword encouraging parents to benefit from the ideas presented here.

Happy reading!

            Marilyn McGinnis

AGREE OR DISAGREE?

AGREE	DISAGREE	
_____	_____	1. Good parents always produce good children.
_____	_____	2. Bad parents always produce bad children.
_____	_____	3. Train up a child in the way he should go and when he grows up he will not depart from it.
_____	_____	4. If a teenager gets involved in drugs, alcoholism or sex, the cause of the problem may be his parents.
_____	_____	5. A parent has in his power the ability to mold a child into a mature, responsible human being.
_____	_____	6. Sin is an outmoded idea. People do not sin — they simply make mistakes.
_____	_____	7. All children who grow up in good homes tend to make right choices later in life.
_____	_____	8. Fairness is very important to children, therefore, all children should be treated alike by their parents.
_____	_____	9. Freedom of choice is a significant factor in a child's development.
_____	_____	10. When I feel guilty, it is because I have done something morally wrong.

1

THE GUILT TRIP

Most of us feel guilty over a number of things God doesn't consider sin.
　　　　　　　Bruce Narramore and Bill Counts
　　　　　　　　　　　　Guilt and Freedom

Tom, the pastor of a small church, is suffering from burnout. He is weak and depressed and has not been able to preach for several weeks. An accumulation of family problems has brought him to the edge.

It is obvious to the congregation, if not to Tom, that he and his family are desperately in need of counseling. Tom and his wife are making some serious mistakes in the way they are raising their children. Their children are spoiled and rebellious and accustomed to getting their own way. The valid guilt Tom and his wife feel over their children's behavior transmits the warning signal that changes need to be made.

Not so the guilt that another parent — Jane — feels. Operating with incorrect medical information, Jane had tried various ways for several years to cope with her two exhaustingly active children. Finally, they were diagnosed accurately as being hyperactive. Had Jane known then what she knows now, she would have done things differently. She still feels guilty about those past years. Should she?

And there's Rod and Anne. Their married son got a divorce. "I imagine you feel quite guilty as a parent because of your son's divorce," a friend said to Rod.

"Not at all," was Rod's reply. "My son makes his own decisions." It shocked this tactless friend who had assumed that a parent's job is never done.

We live in a society and a Christian community that quickly judges parents when children step out of line. Sometimes that judgment is accurate — as in the case of Tom and his wife who lack needed parenting skills. But all too often our children's behavior stems from other factors over which we as parents have little or no control. In those cases, guilt dumped on us is unjustified and robs us of the joy of parenting.

What was your first thought when you heard the news that John Hinckley had shot President Reagan? Did you wonder what his parents had done wrong to produce such behavior in their son? Only when the truth comes out — that these parents had tried every means they knew to help their son, never realizing he was mentally ill — do we grudgingly absolve them of the guilt imposed on them by society.

For several decades parents have been taught that the environment of a child is crucial to his growth and development. And indeed it is. However, there is more to what makes a child tick than the influence of his parents and the home in which he grows up, as important as those are. And parents have little or no control over some of those other factors. How then can they be held responsible for all of what a child becomes? Why should society blame parents for more than their fair share?

Sometimes, though, we parents are quick to blame ourselves when our children step out of line. We hurry to pack our bags for a guilt trip. If your young child misbehaves in front of company, are you hurt and disappointed? If your teenager turns to alcoholism, drugs or immorality, do you shoulder the blame? Do you immediately jump to the conclusion that your child's behavior is a direct result of your parenting? Often, even if we cannot think of anything we have done wrong, we are still sure it is all our fault. We whip out our World's Worst Parent badge and wear it with shame.

If we have wronged one of our children, our guilt is justified and we need to apologize and begin to do things differently. All too often, though, the guilt is not warranted, and we simply allow ourselves to operate under a load of false incrimination.

WHY WE FEEL GUILTY

Let's look at some of the factors that produce false guilt in our lives.

Sometimes we feel guilty because we have set a standard of parenting we can never attain. We become victims of a "superdad/supermom" mentality. Variations on the supermom theme include a "super-working mom" and a "superwife." This type of woman sets a superhuman standard of perfection that says she must be good at everything. She must be a perfect mother, a perfect housekeeper, a perfect career woman and a sexy wife. When she staggers under the load of too much work and not enough hours to get it done, she berates herself for her inefficiency — and she feels guilty.

What about "superdad"? Dave's son Rick smashed up the family car last weekend and smashed himself up as well. When the shock of the accident subsided, Dave realized that Rick's injuries were not serious. Then anger began to build up inside him.

"Now look what you've done, Rick," he shouted through clenched teeth. "When are you going to learn to drive like a responsible person? Do you know how much it's going to cost me to get that car fixed?"

Although Dave won't admit it, he is really more angry with himself than he is with Rick. *If only I hadn't let him use the car last night,* he berates himself. *When will I learn not to give that kid so much responsibility?*

Dave has failed the superdad image he set for himself

and he is taking his guilt out on his son.

"When parents constantly seek perfection as child rearers, they set themselves up for frustration, guilt, and in particular, anger," suggests Joseph Procaccini, an authority on family relationships and co-author of the book, *Parent Burnout*. He notes that as many as 50 percent of parents experience at least the early stages of burnout.[1]

We also can feel guilty when we do not measure up to the expectations of others. These expectations may come from our spouses, our parents, our inlaws or other significant people in our lives. Some people stereotype their mother-in-law as a wicked witch who constantly disapproves of the way they do things. Unfortunately, sometimes the shoe fits.

"I feel so miserable," says Betty, looking both frustrated and angry. "Every time my mother-in-law comes over to the house she picks away at the way we're raising our children. She thinks the curfew we set for Tim is too late and the amount of allowance Cindy gets is outrageous. Nothing I do is right in my mother-in-law's eyes. By the time she leaves I feel guilty — about *everything*. I wish she'd just stay away!"

Mike's father just shook his head in disgust when he saw the new home computer Mike bought for his family. He believes firmly that "a penny saved is a penny earned" and he can't understand why Mike wasted money on a computer.

"I don't know whether to keep the computer or take it back to the store and put the money in the bank," Mike says. "I guess I'll never be as thrifty as my father is. Maybe this thing did cost more than we should spend."

This type of guilt is sneaky because it looks on the surface as if someone else is to blame — Mike's dad and Betty's mother-in-law. In reality, Mike and Betty cause their own guilt when they internalize someone else's standards and make them their own.

Betty actually does a good job with her kids, but she is intimidated by her mother-in-law who thinks kids should be raised as they were thirty years ago. Betty can free herself from false guilt only by living up to her own standards, not someone else's.

Mike is not a spendthrift and he never has been. He believes in the importance of his wife and children learning to use a computer, but now he is torn between fulfilling his own goals as a husband and father and earning his dad's respect.

Both Betty and Mike feel guilty because they desire to do things their own way rather than try to meet their parents' standards.

Sometimes we feel guilty when we do what is right. Now there's a strange one. Doing what is right is supposed to *free* us from guilt, isn't it? Yet at times it does just the opposite — when the happiness of our children is at stake. Some of us feel that our job is to make our children happy. And when we don't, we feel guilty.

"The love trap snaps early and catches a parent in the jaws of feeling the responsibility for making his child happy," write Dave and Jan Stoop in their book, *A Parent's Cry for Help*. "From the time a child first asserts his own will, we struggle with the possibility of our destroying his happiness."

Dave and Jan tell of a time when they had to say no to their son who wanted to use the family car when his own vehicle wasn't running. Because of a bad driving record, Jeff could not be included in the insurance policy for the family car. Finally he accepted the fact that he was going to have to spend a boring evening at home. And his parents felt guilty!

> Every time he walked into the room with a bored look on his face, guilt feelings hit me from every corner. I knew I was doing the right thing, but why did I feel so guilty? Because Jeff was unhappy! And I, like so many other parents, felt it was my job to make him happy. Happiness is always related to a series of happenings. When things run smoothly, we're happy. And I was interfering with Jeff's smooth-running series of happenings.[2]

Another reason for feeling guilty is our false belief that parents alone are responsible for the behavior of their children. What makes us automatically assume we are to blame if our children make wrong choices?

A revolution in knowledge and theories of child-rearing has taken place in the last hundred years. In centuries past, children were not as highly regarded as they are now. They were not studied and analyzed at every turn to see what made them tick.

Child-rearing was based on tradition. Parents raised their children the way they had been raised. Because several generations often lived together, there was always someone around to help parents carry on those traditions.

A WHOLE NEW APPROACH

Then along came Freud and the behavioral psychologists around the turn of the century, and a whole new approach to child-rearing emerged. Instead of viewing children as small adults who should be seen and not heard, we were taught that children are extremely vulnerable, easily damaged by stress and traumatic events. We also were taught, by some, that a child's mind is like a blank slate. If the parents write good things on the slate, the child will turn out well. If they write the wrong things, it is their fault when the child turns out badly. The emphasis fell on rewarding children for their good behavior and on the need for appropriate consequences when they misbehaved.

Has child psychology had an effect on you? Do you have a little chart on your refrigerator door? How many stars have your children collected for drinking their milk, clearing the table or brushing their teeth?

Over the last century, books on child psychology have flooded the market. Much of what these books have to say is good. But the trouble is, they don't all agree. There is no longer a traditional way for parents to raise their children. Instead, many ways have opened up to us, depending upon whose philosophy of child-rearing we espouse.

Each parent must forage through the mass of information on child-rearing and determine which approach he or she will use. Parents today are not likely to be raising their children the way their parents raised them.

This often results in confusion, uncertainty, frustration, and guilt. Why guilt? Because you cannot avoid coming into conflict with someone else's judgment of what is right and what is wrong for your child.

In his book, *Parents in Pain,* John White writes:

> The net result of a deluge of child-rearing articles both religious and secular has been to create two generations of parents who have been anxious, guilty and uncertain of themselves.[3]

Let me make it clear at this point that *Parenting Without Guilt* does not open the door for us to start rationalizing or excusing ourselves for the things we do that are actually wrong. True guilt is important and valuable. It is an emotional gauge that tells us we have blown it. It can lead to repentance and forgiveness and growth. We sense true guilt when the Holy Spirit works in our lives and shows us where we have erred so that we can confess it, profit from the experience, and get on with the business of living.

Jesus told his disciples,

> But the fact of the matter is that it is best for you that I go away, for if I don't, the Comforter won't come. If I do, he will — for I will send him to you. And when he has come he will convince the world of its sin, and of the availability of God's goodness, and of deliverance from judgment (John 16:7,8, TLB).

False guilt, on the other hand, which results from expecting more of ourselves as parents than God expects, is debilitating. It leads to an overdose of introspection, self-pity, despair and even burnout. I actually had a woman tell me that she carries a tremendous load of guilt for the way she raised her daughter. The irony is that she has no reason to feel guilty. Her daughter is a well-adjusted Christian wife and mother. Yet this mother, now a grandmother, cannot forgive herself for real or imagined mistakes of the past.

We must also be aware that freeing ourselves from false guilt does not free us from the pain of seeing our children make wrong choices. However, our pain is multiplied if we add our own false feelings of guilt. Our children are not an extension of ourselves. They are separate individuals who have the same type of sin nature and the same type of will that we have. Sometimes the right thing to do as a parent is to let our children stumble and fall. Sometimes we must be tough in order to help them mature. It is not pleasant to see them suffer but it is not necessarily our fault if they do.

To rid ourselves of false guilt, we must put our parenting into the proper perspective. Our job is an important one and will make a lasting impact on our children. If we seek God's guidance to learn all we can about parenting and do the very best job we can, our children stand a good chance of making right choices when they grow up. If we neglect our responsibility or misuse our authority, our children will pay the price. But we are not the *sole* contributors to our children's destiny.

In succeeding chapters we will look at three factors that, in addition to the home environment, affect how a child will turn out: perception, the sin nature, and freedom of choice. We will discuss how these factors influence a child's ultimate choices, what role parents play in each of these factors, and what parents can and cannot do to bring about change in their children's lives.

But in order to understand more clearly our role as parents in the twentieth century, we first need to look at the revolution in the theories of child-rearing that has taken place in the last few centuries and particularly in the last one hundred years. The perspective of this brief history will help us see why false guilt is such a problem today.

2
WHY GUILT IS A PROBLEM TODAY

Is it remotely possible that any other parents in any other age have had the opportunity to feel as guilty in as many ways as we have? Did they have PG movies? Dinky Donuts Breakfast Cereal? Video games at the checkout counter?

I mean, could "Ozzie and Harriet" have survived the two-paycheck marriage? Could "Leave It to Beaver" have flourished in an era of joint custody?

Glen Collins
How to Be a Guilty Parent

When I was born, my mother tells me, a government book on child-rearing advocated not hugging or kissing babies. Having seen children come down with colds and other symptoms caught from "kissy" adults, my parents reasoned that this was good advice. After all, their friends were reading the same book.

So for the first two years of my life my parents neither hugged nor kissed me. Finally my mother could stand it no longer. She threw the book out, picked me up and began to make up for lost time.

When my own children were small, Dr. Spock's book on child-rearing had had its heyday and was being replaced by new "authorities" on child-rearing who defended their own position by attacking Dr. Spock. About the time you think you've done a pretty good job with your kids, a new book comes along with an opposing view.

Are there really that many ways to raise children? Or is there really only one tried and true way (*my* way, of course)? How did we get to this point in history and how does this great variety of child-rearing methods produce false guilt? In order to understand where we are today we need to take a brief look back.

Since the beginning of time when God commanded Adam and Eve to be fruitful, multiply and replenish the earth, mankind has been doing just that. In a largely agrarian society, big families were needed to help till the soil and harvest the crops.

In the Old Testament, parents were admonished to teach their children the law and to bring them up as God-fearing adults. The Greek philosophers of the fourth and fifth centuries B.C., on the other hand, believed in the supremacy of the state and devised educational methods that prepared their children for state-approved occupations. Children were loved and desired, but discipline was usually quick and severe if a child stepped out of line.

> The family fulfilled a function; it ensured the transmission of life, property and names; but it did not penetrate very far into human sensibility.[1]

There was little if any interest in how children's thoughts, attitudes and behavior developed.

THE CHRISTIAN VIEW OF CHILDREN

When Jesus Christ entered the scene, He taught that every person has *equal* value in God's eyes, whether young or old. Often Christ's teachings were negatively interpreted because of the influence of the culture. An example of this can be found in Mark 10:13-16 when the children came to see Jesus.

> They brought children for him to touch; and the disciples scolded them for it. But when Jesus saw this he

was indignant, and said to them, "Let the children come to me; do not try to stop them; for the kingdom of God belongs to such as these. I tell you, whoever does not accept the kingdom of God like a child will never enter it." And he put his arms around them, laid his hands upon them, and blessed them (NEB).

The disciples, influenced by the culture and society in which they lived, did not comprehend the worth of the individual, including children. In a way, they were saying, "Get those little people out of here. Jesus is too busy for children."

Jesus was indignant at the disciples' insensitivity to the children's feelings. He demanded that they be brought to Him. With His loving embrace and verbal blessing of the children, He taught a powerful lesson to the adults.

On another occasion, when the arrogant disciples showed concern over who would be the greatest in heaven, Jesus used an unpretentious child as an example of the humility needed to enter the kingdom. The disciples must have tumbled over in shock when Jesus pressed the matter even further:

> "Whoever receives one such child in my name receives me. But if a man is a cause of stumbling to one of these little ones who have faith in me, it would be better for him to have a millstone hung around his neck and be drowned in the depths of the sea" (Matthew 18:5-6, NEB).

SOCIETY'S CHANGING VIEW OF CHILDREN

Through the centuries, society's attitude toward children gradually changed. In *Centuries of Childhood,* Phillippe Ariès gives us a picture of the progression of adult interest in children, often reflected in art and literature.

In the medieval world there seems to have been little regard for childhood either in art or literature. In art, children were usually depicted as *little adults* with the features, body structure and clothing of an adult, but smaller in size. In literature, children acted with the valor and strength of adult warriors. Only Greek art presented realistic representations of children.

Gradually a growing consciousness of the individuality of children developed. "There can be no doubt," writes Ariès, "that the importance accorded to the child's personality was linked with the growing influence of Christianity on life and manners.[2]

By the beginning of the seventeenth century portraits of historic children apart from their parents became common. "Henceforth he would be depicted by himself and for himself: this was the great novelty of the seventeenth century."[3]

EARLY DEVELOPERS OF CHILD PSYCHOLOGY

As interest in children grew, men and women from various fields — philosophy, medicine, psychoanalysis — began to study children and share their views about them. Out of these studies came the development of child psychology as we know it today, each one influencing the standards of child-rearing.

The English philosopher *John Locke* was one of the first writers to influence people's thinking about children. His treatise, *Some Thoughts Concerning Education,* published in 1693, was a collection of letters to a friend advising him on how to raise his son to be an English gentleman. Locke, who never married but was well-educated and tutored children, disapproved of apprenticing children; he felt it was the parents' responsibility to rear their own children. He opposed the heavy discipline and the dogmatic instruction of the schools of his day. Rather, he believed that sensory experience was vital for learning and felt children should be allowed to express their feelings. He urged the reader to study children and find out what they were like in order to make their education more useful. Locke believed that parents must establish their authority early in a child's life, but he resisted corporal punishment except in cases of obstinacy or rebellion.

> ... if the mind be curbed and humbled too much in children, if their spirits be abased and broken much by too strict a hand over them, they lose all their vigour and industry and are in a worse state than the former.[4]

Locke's views on society's responsibility to alter children's undesirable behavior laid the foundation for modern principles of behavior modification.

THREE REASONS FOR THE GROWING INTEREST IN CHILDREN

After centuries of largely ignoring children, why did society suddenly begin to take an interest in studying and understanding them? Three factors contributed to that interest. One of them was the new regard for *education*.

There has always been some form of education for children, but much of it in centuries past was either religious in nature or vocationally oriented. In the Western world children entered an apprenticeship at the age of six or seven and were trained for a particular trade. The Industrial Revolution of the eighteenth century created a new interest in providing a broader education for children.

> The Industrial Revolution created a world with complex economics and complicated occupational roles, roles that could not be learned by imitation and example, as in an apprenticeship. A rapidly changing society called for people who had breadth of understanding and who had a good range of social and intellectual skills, people who could work together as members of organizations, initiate and conduct civic enterprises, and perform a variety of functions in different social settings. The schooling that the elite had been providing for their children and young people served as a first model. Literacy was a first goal in this education, followed by understanding of the world, its customs, traditions, and practices. Thus the modern school curriculum was born.

The harsh family discipline of the times was at first carried over into the schools virtually unchanged, but wiser schoolmasters soon realized that horses led to water do not necessarily drink, even when beaten.[5]

As society's interest in the importance of educating children grew, so did a new interest in the child himself.

Henceforth it was recognized that the child was not ready for life, and that he had to be subjected to a special treatment, a sort of quarantine, before he was allowed to join the adults. This new concern about education would gradually install itself in the heart of society and transform it from top to bottom. The family ceased to be simply an institution for the transmission of a name and an estate — it assumed a moral and spiritual function, it molded bodies and souls.[6]

In addition to the influence of education, Watson and Lindgren, authors of *Psychology of the Child,* suggest two more reasons for the growing interest in children. According to Watson and Lindgren, the psychology of children, which resulted from the interest and study of children, is one of the by-products of *our struggle to become democratic.* In a society where an individual's worth is tied to his station in life, a child's status is not very great. In a true democracy, however, each individual, including the child, is regarded as a person of worth.

The third reason for the growth of child psychology is *our desire as adults to understand ourselves.*

One of the paths to self-discovery lies through child psychology; through our study of the child, we believe that we can find some of the keys to the mystery that is ourselves — who we are. We all realize that we are infinitely more than we were at birth, and our exploration of the events and experiences of infancy and childhood holds the promise of filling in the gap between ourselves at birth and what we are today. We examine the accounts of these events and experiences in search of ourselves, in search of explanations for our successes and failures, our inhibitions and capacities, our potentialities for pleasure and sorrow.[7]

NATURE VERSUS NURTURE

If all theories of child psychology could be reduced to the simplest common denominator, it would be *nature versus nurture*. Those on the nature side believe that a child's behavior is predetermined by his nature or heredity. Environment has little or no influence on how the child will turn out.

The Puritans held that children are born evil because they have inherited a sin nature from their father Adam. Much of the harsh discipline of the Puritan era can be attributed to their belief that a child's wicked ways must be curbed.

Rousseau, on the other hand, believed that children are born inherently good. This is the view held by humanists today and is prevalent in all aspects of our society. The humanist view of man holds that:

> The biologically determined inner nature of the human consists of basic needs, emotions, and capacities that are either neutral or positively *good*. They certainly are not evil. . . . Therefore, the goal of guiding child development is one of fostering the expression of the child's inner nature. This task is a difficult and crucial one because the inner essence of the child's personality is not very hardy. It is delicate and easily damaged by unfavorable experiences.[8]

On the nurture side, John Locke believed that "at birth a child's mind is a void, an unmarked page or *tabula rasa* on which the contents of the mind are sketched by the child's experiences as he grows up.[9] The experiences a child has as he is growing up determine how he will turn out.

Both sides of the nature/nurture debate have greatly influenced our views on child-rearing.

THE GOOD NEWS — AND THE BAD

The study of children has provided us with an enormous volume of information, theories and opinions about children and how they should be brought up. But, having traded authoritarianism for a more democratic method of child-rearing, we have also lost the simplicity of the "one way to raise children" of our forebears. No longer do we parents raise our children the way our parents raised us. Some parents, in fact, try very hard *not* to raise their children the way they were brought up.

Parenting styles now range from a few authoritarian parents who maintain rigid control over their children to permissive parents who pretty much let their children call the shots. The rest of us struggle for some kind of middle road between the two extremes.

Sifting the good from the bad in the plethora of advice on parenting, and choosing that which best benefits our children as individuals, is an enormous task — one that calls for a great deal of wisdom and discernment. If we lean too heavily on the nature side of the coin, we may become legalistic and unfeeling in our approach to parenting. If we move too far into the environmentalist camp, we may easily push our role as parents out of perspective. The result will be an enormous load of false guilt when we do not measure up to our expectations of the kind of environment we should provide for our children.

Many of us, sad to say, have listened more to the nurturing side of child psychology than to the nature side. We recognize the importance of our input into our children, but we push that line of reasoning too far. Subtle and not-so-subtle influences have convinced us that we and we alone are responsible for how our children turn out.

The *authoritarian parent* of centuries past, who had no qualms about beating the devil out of his child, has been replaced by the *anxious parent* who fears the effect that even the normal ups and downs of family life will have on his child.

- If we disagree over something and express our feel-

ings in front of the children, we feel guilty for fear we have upset them.
- If we discipline them, we have a nagging fear that we may be curbing their creative urges.
- If they make a wrong decision, especially a serious one, we are racked with guilt because somewhere we failed to write "the right thing" on their minds.

"Why should mothers feel this burden of guilt?" asks Lynn Caine, author of *What Did I Do Wrong?* "Even for circumstances over which we have absolutely no control? Because," she says, "we have come to believe what we have been told."

> As Betty Friedan observed some two decades ago in *The Feminine Mystique,* popularizers of Freudian psychology suddenly discovered in the 1940s that mothers were to blame for almost everything wrong with the American family and people. "In every case history of troubled child," she wrote, "of alcoholic, suicidal, schizophrenic, psychopathic, neurotic adult; impotent, homosexual male; frigid, promiscuous female; ulcerous, asthmatic and otherwise disturbed American, could be found a mother."
>
> Modern medical and psychological research tells us that this sweeping mother blaming is nonsense. But the damage was done, and the wounds remain. Mother has been judged and found guilty, just as I have judged and blamed myself.[10]

To maintain our perspective, we need to look at the complete picture of what makes a child do what he does. The home environment is an important factor in a child's development; there's no doubt about it. But it is not the only factor that affects how a child will turn out. As Caine explains it:

> Partly through my own children, partly from other mothers, and partly from researchers I respect, I have found a growing body of evidence to suggest that mother may have only a limited influence for good or bad. No one can predict or determine the way a child is going to turn out. There are very few useful rules on how to bring up healthy, well-adjusted children, and even when

these few rules are followed there is no guarantee that they will prove effective. Even experts have disturbed children. Offspring who look like sure losers turn out winners; early winners turn out losers in the long run. Adversity may hurt children, strengthen children, or have little to do with their development. Children are far more resilient than we have been led to believe by quasi Freudians and well-meaning experts who give us prescriptions for raising our families; and we do not understand why it is that some youngsters scar easily and others, miraculously, do not scar even under apparently devastating conditions.

But one thing is clear: Emotional well-being does not depend on mothers alone. I do not mean to minimize the mother's role in shaping her child. But there are many other factors involved in personality development and character structure, including of course the father, position in the family, genetics, temperament, health, intelligence, peers, teachers, society, economics, and just plain luck.[11]

How should we respond to the idea that we parents have less control over what happens to our children than we first believed? We can choose to feel helpless and unnecessary. Or we can heave a sigh of relief that the burden of parenting is lighter than we had imagined.

Nowhere in this book will you find the role of the parent diminished. God has called us to be all that a Christian father and mother should be — and He has promised to help us accomplish the job. But because we are God's handiwork, His creation and His alone, we are complex creatures. We are not robots who need to have our computers programmed. Many factors are at work to help us determine who we really are and what our purpose on earth really is.

We parents are a major factor in shaping our children's lives. I cannot emphasize that enough. But we are not the only factors. It is God's job to work in our children's lives — in areas where we are not responsible to accomplish what we as parents cannot do on our own. That's the whole point of salvation, isn't it? We cannot provide salvation for another person. Only God can do that. We can testify to God's reliability and encourage our children to put Him first in their lives. But the ultimate outcome is between the child and God.

When my children were still quite young I came to the conclusion that parenting is a team effort. As a parent I can't possibly teach my children all the things they will need for maturity and growth. Why? Because, as a human being, I have my limitations. I try to do my very best. But there are other people in this world who will also play a significant role in my children's lives — grandparents, teachers, peers, friends. I am relieved to know that my husband and I are not alone in parenting.

In the next three chapters we will look at three factors that greatly affect how a child will turn out — factors over which parents have little or no control. Those factors are *perception, the sin nature,* and *freedom of choice.* We will discuss the part we as parents play in each of these factors, and when we must back off and let God do His work in His own way.

3

THE POWER OF PERCEPTION

You can guide a child, but he will form his own perceptions. However, in order to guide your child adequately, your own perceptions must be accurate.
                                                M.M.

When I was a child growing up in Washington state, I was particularly impressed with a high school girl several years older than I. Sue had been severely crippled by polio as a child. Every morning I watched her hobble from her home to the bus stop. She was a cheerful, gregarious girl. In fact, as I recall, her nickname was "Sunny."

Somewhere along the line, "Sunny" had learned to think beyond the limitations of her body and to perceive herself as a person of worth. As a result, she was well liked by her many high school friends.

In contrast to "Sunny," twenty-two-year-old Will, who was also crippled by polio at an early age, was never able to accept his disability. Despite all the love and care his parents gave him, he took his own life.

How a child perceives himself and events around him plays a crucial part in his development. This perception has a definite effect on how he will turn out in later life.

Where does perception come from? To find an answer we must return to the nature versus nurture theories of psychology. In *The Power of Your Perceptions,* William V. Arnold points out that our perceptions come from *both* nature and nurture.

We are endowed at birth with certain characteristics which predetermine how we will perceive the world. Some people are extroverts, viewing the world through other people. Some people are introverts, viewing the world through their own inner resources. Others perceive the world in terms of what is real — the facts and details get their attention first. Another group views the world in terms of what is possible. "These are the dreamers, the visionaries, the ones who are more fascinated with concepts and ideas than with facts and details," says Arnold.[1]

On the nurture side, Arnold points out that we learn early in life from our environment whom we can trust, what we are capable of doing, and, particularly in our teen years, who we are. We learn which adults in our environment or which types of people are trustworthy, and we carry that perception with us for many years. We learn what we are capable of doing by the way the adults in our lives treat us. We either perceive ourselves as capable, but with limitations, or we view ourselves as never doing things quite well enough, never quite measuring up to the expectations of the adults around us. As the adolescent tries to determine who he is, part of that concern centers on whether he is trustworthy and how he perceives himself as a person of worth.

HEREDITY AND PERCEPTION

In the biblical story of the man born blind, genetics had dealt the man a cruel blow. From the moment he left his mother's womb, he had never been able to see.

Jesus and His disciples spotted the man at the same time. Before Jesus had a chance to speak, His disciples posed a question: "Rabbi, who sinned, this man or his parents? Why was he born blind?" (John 9:2 NEB).

"Is it this man's nature that caused him to be blind?" the disciples wanted to know. "Or is his blindness the result of his parents' sin nature?"

Why is one person born blind and another not? Why is one person born with straight, healthy limbs, another with serious deformities? Why does one person have an I.Q. over 150 and another have Down's Syndrome?

In 1854 a monk named Gregor Mendel asked himself the same kinds of questions, and he began to look for some answers. In the garden of the monastery where he lived, in what is now part of Czechoslovakia, he carefully recorded his experiments with growing peas.

Why, he wondered, did smooth-coated peas produce both smooth-coated and wrinkle-coated peas? Why did tall pea plants sometimes produce dwarf plants? Why did plants grown from yellow seeds sometimes produce green seeds instead? In these early beginnings, small glimmers of understanding began to grow as man's understanding of genetics began to emerge.

Today we know that we inherit genes and chromosomes from our parents that affect our looks, the way our body functions, our intelligence, sex, abilities, talents and our length of life. These in turn affect our personality, temperament, behavior, and, in some cases, may even be a direct cause of criminal behavior.

Do you wonder how heredity affects what your children do? Try an experiment. Choose one of your children (older elementary through teenage) and go to the doorway of that child's room. Look around the room and see what you can discover about that child. Look past the unmade bed or the general mess and try for a moment to see your child reflected in that room. Then think beyond that room to additional possessions your child may have in other parts of the house. Record your observations on a piece of paper.

What colors of paint and/or wallpaper are used in the decor of the room? Who chose those colors — you or your child?

What hobbies or interests does your child have —

stamp collecting, model trains, needlework, musical instruments, sports?

What books are favorites?

As I look at my nine-and-a-half-year-old daughter's room I observe these things:
- Pink flowered wallpaper, a blue rug, a canopy bed.
- A Girl Scout uniform in her closet.
- Library books reflecting a newfound interest in reading for pleasure.
- A Michael Jackson poster shoved behind her desk. (She liked him when she bought the poster a few weeks ago — or was it peer pressure? Now she doesn't.)
- Doll collection — probably as much my collection as hers because she isn't terribly interested in dolls.

In other parts of the house I find:
- Piano in the living room where she practices her piano lessons.
- Calico cat named Kiki — her prized possession.
- Two recently acquired rabbits in a hutch in the backyard.
- Jar of peanut butter in the refrigerator — the fifth food group at our house. Without it she would go through withdrawal.

Now divide your findings into these four categories:

1. *Parent's Choice* (largely suggested by the parent with little if any agreement or interest on the part of the child);

2. *Parent/Child Choice* (parent suggested but child agreed);

3. *Peer Pressure* (the child has this or does this because all his/her friends do);

4. *Child's Choice* (represents the child's interest or ability).

Some may overlap, but try to choose the category that is most appropriate.

My list for my daughter looks like this:

1. Parent's Choice:	**2. Parent/Child Choice:**
Bedroom rug	Bedroom color scheme
Girl Scouts	Doll collection

3. **Peer Pressure:**
   Michael Jackson poster

4. **Child's Choice:**
   Canopy bed
   Wallpaper
   Cat and rabbits
   Piano lessons
   Library books
   Peanut butter

The list for a teenager's room will look quite different from that of an elementary school child. Here is one father's humorous analysis of his eighteen-year-old son's bedroom and possessions:

Item:	Dad's Comments:
Loft bed	My son got this idea from a friend. We built it together. It resulted in a unique bedroom and provided more floor space for his clothes.
Bird	He wanted a bird about eight years ago. Grandfather provided it. Mom and Dad didn't think this was the best way to feed our cat, nor did we feel that the cat should be given away (son's idea). Finally agreed to allow him to have bird with stipulation that cat remain. He would need to keep the bird away from the cat. The bird is still alive and well.
Desk	Parents working hard at improving son's grades.
Barbells	Son wants to stay in shape for the girls.
Recliner chair	Son's idea. Old chair. Good place to talk on phone.
Brown walls	Son's idea. He selected color and did all the painting.
Trumpet	Parents want to foster music. Son has made it his own. Many friendships have resulted from his involvement in band at school. (Also made going to school tolerable).
Computer	Parents' idea. (Too much money being spent on arcade games.) Son enjoys

	it and has learned a lot.
Dresser	Part of great-grandparents' bedroom set. Used by me. Son could care less.

The father categorizes his son's possessions as follows:

1. **Parent's Choice:**
   Desk
   Dresser
2. **Parent/Child Choice:**
   Trumpet
   Computer
3. **Peer Pressure:**
   Barbells
4. **Child's Choice:**
   Bird
   Recliner chair
   Brown walls
   Loft bed

After you record your observations of your own child, study the categories. How much of what your child has and does is a reflection of his or her heredity (interests, talents, abilities?) How much is a reflection of peer pressure? How much is a reflection of *your* heredity more than your child's?

Now consider what your child's self perception might be in light of these four categories. What perception can a child have who is allowed very little freedom of expression, whose parents make all his decisions? If parents continually put down the child's ideas in favor of their own, the child may feel that his own God-given interests and abilities are of little worth. Hence, *he* is worthless.

What perception might a child have if most of what he does or has is the result of peer pressure? Chances are the child finds his own identity only in the identity of others. Without them, he is lost.

What perception might a child have of himself based on his parents' reactions to the things he considers an extension of himself — his choice of room color, his clothes, his artistic or athletic interests? (Men often view their cars as extensions of themselves and women their homes. Why shouldn't a child have similar views?)

When we moved into our home, the carpet in my daughter's room was old and ugly. It was some time before we could afford to buy her a new carpet. Without thinking of the consequences, many nights I'd go into her room to bid goodnight and say, "This room is so ugly, Shana, we've *got* to do something about it."

Finally, one night she said, "Am I really that bad, Mommy?" I realized for the first time that she considered her room an extension of herself. If I thought her room was ugly, then in her young mind I must have the same opinion of her.

Every child deserves the right to have his God-given interests and abilities — his heredity — taken seriously by those who care about him.

While heredity determines how we will look and what our interests and abilities will be, it is our *perception* of our body and mind that affects how we will behave.

Over the years we have developed some stereotypes for various bodily features and intelligence. We call people with narrow-set eyes shifty, those with a receding chin weak, and those with a sharp thin nose cruel. Tall people tend to command more respect than short people. If we believe these stereotypes, we will tend to treat others and ourselves accordingly.

Yet many people do not fit those stereotypes at all. My child psychology teacher in college was a little bit of a mite, but she had *no* difficulty commanding respect. A pastor friend has a receding chin, but he is one of the strongest Christians I know.

Certainly our genetic make-up does predispose us to susceptibility to certain diseases (on the negative side), and to certain talents and abilities (on the positive side). Medical science is constantly researching new ways to treat — and even prevent — inherited and non-hereditary diseases. But the only real control we adults have over our children's heredity is simply to not have children at all.

Many parents try to treat each child individually, as a person of worth, regardless of physical appearance or abilities. But sometimes a child chooses to view himself in a negative way and there is nothing we can do about it. By the same token, some children choose to view themselves in a positive light despite their physical or mental limitations. We can encourage them, pray for them and praise them. But ultimately how they will view themselves is their decision alone.

PERCEPTION AND TRAUMATIC EVENTS

Our perception of ourselves and other people, and our resulting behavior, is also based on events that happen outside ourselves. Traumatic events such as the death of a loved one or divorce can produce a distorted view of ourselves and those around us.

Frequently children of divorced parents perceive themselves to be the cause of their parents' divorce. They reason that if they had been a better child or done more things to please their parents, then their parents would not have divorced. Until we help a child work through this erroneous perception, he will view himself in a negative light.

A friend says that when he was a small child his mother had to work in order for the family to survive. He was well cared for when his mother was at work. But in his young mind, he perceived her going to work as abandonment. For years, after becoming an adult, he was afraid to get close to women for fear they would abandon him like he thought his mother had. Apparently, he is the only family member who perceived the situation in this way.

Should his mother have stayed home and not worked and let the family starve? Certainly not. Most likely she didn't know what was going on inside his head, for children seldom tell us everything they are thinking.. The good news is that my friend overcame his fear of women in later years.

Each of us perceives things in our own way, based on such factors as our age, our past experiences, our sex and our expectations. Good times and bad times happen in every family. As parents, we cannot control how our children will perceive those events. We can only hope and pray that their perceptions will be more positive than negative. Even if a child's perception of something is negative, it's not the end of the world. God is in the business of helping each of us grow and expand in our capacity to love and be loved.

No two children will perceive an event in precisely the same way. One may see it as a positive force in his life. Another may see it as negative. That is something over which parents have little or no control, simply because we cannot read our children's minds.

WHAT ARE YOUR PERCEPTIONS?

You can guide your children, but they will form their own perceptions. However, in order to guide your children adequately your own perceptions must be accurate.

Who do you consider trustworthy in this world? Are you generally a "trusting soul" except when the facts indicate you should be wary? Or did your early childhood experiences leave you distrustful of most people or of certain ethnic or social groups? Are you passing these same perceptions on to your children, either consciously or unconsciously?

How do you view your own capabilities? Do you have a healthy self-esteem, viewing both your abilities and limitations in a realistic way? Or do you constantly try to build yourself up in your own eyes by criticizing other people? Do your children never quite measure up — academically, physically, mentally, or socially? Will your criticism affect their perceptions of their own self-worth?

Who are you in your own eyes? Do you see yourself as a creature of worth placed on earth by a loving God who sent His son to die in order that you might live? Do you really believe that God loves you unconditionally? Or do you feel that you never quite measure up in God's eyes or anyone else's for that matter? Do you believe God loves your children unconditionally? Do you love your children unconditionally? In what ways are you conveying this to them?

The old adage that you can only lead a person as far as you have gone yourself is certainly true in the area of perception. If you wonder what perceptions you are transmitting to your children, ask them. You may be surprised at their answers.

We have seen in this chapter how a child's perception of his own heredity and of outside events can shape his behavior. And we have seen that parents have little (in some cases no) control over his perception. But there is another area we need to consider if we are to rid ourselves of false guilt. We must recognize that each child is born with a sin nature which — apart from the saving power of Jesus Christ — predisposes him to varying degrees of negative behavior.

FOR FURTHER READING

Amram Scheinfeld, *Heredity In Humans,* (New York: J. B. Lippincott, 1972).

Alvin and Virginia Silverstein, *The Genetics Explosion,* (New York: Four Winds Press, 1980).

Margaret O. Hyde, *The New Genetics,* (New York: Franklin Watts, Inc., 1974).

Amram Scheinfeld, *Why You Are You,* (New York: Association Press, 1970).

William V. Arnold, *The Power Of Your Perceptions,* (Philadelphia: The Westminster Press, 1984).

4

WHATEVER HAPPENED TO SIN?

The Devil's cleverest wile is to convince us that he does not exist.

Charles Baudelaire

Our children are still young enough to enjoy hearing about our experiences as children. Sometimes they hear about the good things we did, sometimes about the bad.

At bedtime one evening something prompted my husband to tell our boys about a time when he had foolishly stolen a magazine from a store and was caught. He was humiliated over the incident but was glad in later years that he had been caught.

A few minutes after he left the boys' room, a small voice called out in the dark, "Mom."

I hear that word often after lights are out so I was not eager to respond. Eventually, when I did, I found a tearful boy confessing a lie he had told some time back. I don't know if it had been eating away at him, or if he had forgotten it until then. But the Lord had used my husband's confession of sin to bring a small boy to repentance for his own wrongdoing.

IS THERE REALLY A SIN NATURE?

Are we really born with a sin nature? (Theologians call it the doctrine of original sin.) Or is the idea just a throwback to some Victorian era that we should erase from our memory? In a world of sophisticated technology and scientific wonders, isn't the idea of sin just a little bit old-fashioned? Theologians and philosophers have struggled with the issue of man's innate goodness or badness for centuries.

As human beings we do not like to admit that we are sinners. Or that our children are. We would much rather view ourselves as self-made men and women who occasionally make mistakes but who are really good persons underneath. Because of this desire to see ourselves as good, mankind has tried to explain away sin for centuries. While there are many variations, ideas about sin are generally polarized around two opposite points of view. Let's look at them.

1. *"There is no such thing as original sin."* This is the "every day in every way I'm getting better and better" philosophy. According to this philosophy, people make mistakes but they are certainly not all bad. This view was developed in the fifth century A.D. by a British monk named Pelagius and a Roman lawyer named Celestius. Pelagius believed that man did not inherit a sin nature from Adam. Rather, he believed that man could achieve a sinless life by an act of will which resulted in salvation by good works. He believed the law, the gospel, and the grace of God could aid attainment of salvation, but these were not absolutely necessary for salvation.

Although the Pelagian view of sin was ruled unorthodox and, therefore, incorrect by the council of Ephesus in A.D. 431, it is a recurring theme still found in liberal theology and many churches and cults today.

In everyday practice, the Pelagian view considers man capable of being good simply by continually making right choices. Man becomes his own "savior," capable of earning his own salvation.

Is man really capable of never sinning? Not according

to the apostle Paul:

> I don't understand myself at all, for I really want to do what is right, but I can't. I do what I don't want to — what I hate. I know perfectly well that what I am doing is wrong, and my bad conscience proves that I agree with these laws I am breaking. But I can't help myself, because I'm no longer doing it. It is sin inside me that is stronger than I am that makes me do these evil things (Romans 7:15-17, TLB).

It takes truly honest people to admit that when push comes to shove, we are really incapable of making ourselves become what we want to be. It takes an outside source — someone who has greater power than the sin nature within us which seeks to control us — to bring about a change which Christians call the new birth. This leads us, of course, to the second point of view:

2. "*Man is a sinner from birth and can only find personal salvation from sin through Christ.*" Augustine, who lived from A.D. 354-430, was one of the most influential of all the early church fathers. He believed firmly in the doctrine of original sin. Perhaps the reason he held so strongly to the biblical evidence for sin, and disputed the Pelagian view so soundly, was because he had experienced sin so deeply. As a young man he had lived an exceedingly sinful and immoral life, all the while searching for what he considered to be the truth. It was not until he read Romans 13:13,14 that his search for truth was rewarded.

> Be decent and true in everything you do so that all can approve your behavior. Don't spend your time in wild parties and getting drunk or in adultery and lust, or fighting, or jealousy. But ask the Lord Jesus Christ to help you live as you should, and don't make plans to enjoy evil (TLB).

A teacher by profession, Augustine was eventually made the chief bishop of North Africa and his influence as theologian, defender of the faith and writer is still felt today. "Thou has formed us for Thyself," he wrote, "and our hearts are restless till they find their rest in Thee."

During the Reformation Martin Luther disagreed strongly with the Roman Catholic teachings that salvation was obtainable by works and that the Pope had the power to forgive sins. He believed that man was totally corrupted by sin and had no power to save himself. He also reaffirmed the biblical teaching that only God can forgive sins.

Out of the Reformation came a renewed belief in the doctrine of original sin and the need for personal salvation by faith alone, not by works. Out of the Renaissance, on the other hand, came a new interest in humanity with its emphasis on human reason and the goodness of humanity, known today as humanism.

WHERE DID OUR SIN NATURE COME FROM?

We were sitting around a table in the primary department at our church discussing the fact that God and Satan are not exactly the best of friends. In fact, to put it mildly, they are enemies. Satan stands for all that is evil. God stands for all that is good.

"Then why," asked one of the little second-grade boys, "did God make Satan in the first place?"

That question has plagued philosophers and theologians for centuries.

The origin of sin lies with Satan (also called the devil or Lucifer) who was one of God's angels in heaven. Satan decided that he wanted to be equal with God and that was his big mistake.

> How are you fallen from heaven, O Lucifer, son of the morning! . . . For you said to yourself, . . . "I will climb to the highest heavens and be like the Most High" (Isaiah 14:12-14, TLB).

Because of his act of insurrection Satan and his followers were thrown out of heaven and the great war between good and evil began.

Why God didn't kick Satan out of existence altogether remains one of the mysteries of the universe. Yet theologians who believe in original sin agree that sin is necessary because God's mercy and justice could not be shown if there were no sin. Mercy could not be demonstrated if there were no situations warranting God's merciful intervention. Justice would not be necessary if there were no situations in which injustice threatened to prevail.

But wouldn't it be easier if God had just zapped Satan and made him a good guy again? Of course it would, but God's nature is such that He isn't in the zapping business. He is in the business of allowing us to make choices. It is only in the process of making right choices that we grow to be more like Him.

Sin next appears in the Garden of Eden when God made Adam and Eve. He gave them every part of His creation to enjoy. The only thing He asked was that they not eat of the fruit of one particular tree in the garden. Satan entered the picture at that point and urged Eve to go ahead and eat of the fruit. "God knows," he said, "that the instant you eat it you will become like him" (Genesis 3:5, TLB).

Satan was unable to obtain equality with God so he deluded Eve into thinking she could have it. In reality, however, disobeying God made her less like God — not more — since God is sinless. Eve disobeyed God and so did Adam. The same tendency toward sin has been passed from generation to generation.

> Wherefore, as by one man sin entered into the world, and death by sin; and so death passed upon all men, for that all have sinned (Romans 5:12, KJV).

THAT'S NOT FAIR!

"But that's not fair," you say. "Why should I have to

pay for what someone else did before me?"

You're right. It isn't fair. But it's a fact. Is it fair that I was born into a family that has a tendency toward diabetes? Or that you inherited a particular defect or disease from your parents? In order to survive and lead productive lives, people with handicaps learn early in life to accept their limitations as a fact of life and to go on from there. Denial won't work. Neither will a morbid preoccupation with their infirmity.

Just as some inherited diseases ultimately lead to death, so our sin nature leads to spiritual death. For sin separates us from God.

> Listen now! The Lord isn't too weak to save you. And he isn't getting deaf! He can hear you when you call! But the trouble is that your sins have cut you off from God. Because of sin he has turned his face away from you and will not listen anymore (Isaiah 59:1,2, TLB).

Sin is defined in Scripture as "the transgression of the law" (1 John 3:4, KJV). It is failure to keep the laws which God has set before us. The law is the written expression of God's holiness — the steps necessary to be holy as God is holy.

IS THERE NO HOPE?

Are we destined to be forever separated from God because of our sin? Certainly not. What a cruel God we would have if He allowed sin to enter our lives and then did nothing about it. The central theme of the entire Bible is that Jesus Christ entered the world to save us from our sins. In society, if a law is broken, a penalty must be paid. So it is in God's world. Jesus Christ, by His death on the cross nearly two thousand years ago, paid the penalty for all our sin. He asks that we admit our sin and our need of someone to save us and then He asks us to commit our lives to Him as Savior and Lord.

When Jesus Christ comes into our lives with all His

love and power, we cross the bridge from hopelessness, despair and self-effort to hope and joy and peace. It doesn't mean we will never again sin, for growth takes time. It does mean that when we confess our sin to God, He will forgive us and go on loving us as if we had never sinned.

> Greater love hath no man than this, that a man lay down his life for his friends (John 15:13, KJV).

WHAT'S ALL THIS GOT TO DO WITH PARENTING?

Every child is born into this world with a sin nature. How that child allows God to deal with that sin nature largely determines how the child will turn out when he grows up. Except for our influence, we as parents have little control over this because it is an *individual* decision.

As parents we can bring our children up in the "nurture and admonition of the Lord." But we cannot force them to reject sin and follow Christ. The individual child must make that decision.

But there are some things we can do to point our children in the right direction. And these things are extremely important.

First, we must make certain that we ourselves have found forgiveness for our sins through Jesus Christ. The parent whose sins have been forgiven by God and who lives at peace with the maker of the universe, sets a powerful example for his or her children.

Once we have established that right relationship with God, we have the power of God's Holy Spirit within us to help us do the right job of parenting. God has promised that He will never leave us nor forsake us. No matter how difficult our situation may be, He is right there beside us to help and to comfort. In a society where people turn to drugs, alcohol and other forms of abuse to try to rid themselves of inner turmoil, the example of a person whose feet are placed on solid ground through Jesus Christ speaks volumes.

The first beatitude in Jesus' Sermon on the Mount says,

> Blessed are they who know their spiritual poverty, for theirs is the kingdom of heaven (Matthew 5:3, Berkeley).

The reward for spiritual honesty is that we will inherit the kingdom of heaven and in so doing we will set a powerful example for our children.

Second, we must point our children to the one who can save them from their sins. We do this through reading and discussing the Bible at home, by taking (not sending) our children to Sunday school and church, and through countless little daily conversations when we can show them God's love at work in the universe and in our individual lives.

One of the best ways we can point our children to the Lord is through honesty. Think for a moment about how many problems in this world are based on dishonesty. Cliff and Jill are having marital problems because Cliff can't hold down a job and the family is constantly one step away from poverty. Cliff refuses to admit it's because he has a drinking problem.

Sue and her daughter Melissa are continually at loggerheads because Melissa is running with the wrong crowd and Sue doesn't like it. Melissa won't admit that her friends are immature and reckless.

Dave is frequently angry at his boss and broods for days on end. He feels discriminated against because he is often passed over at promotion time. Dave won't admit that his own emotional immaturity is keeping him from being promoted.

I am disturbed by parents who feel that it's permissible to lie to their children under certain circumstances. For example, they give the family dog away because they don't want it anymore, yet they tell the children someone has stolen it. What happens to their credibility when the neighbor boy tells them he saw their parents take the dog to the pound?

Or when the father's job requires a move to a new location, they tell the children that if they don't like the new house they'll move back to the old one. Does hoping for something that will never happen really save a child from the pain of separation when the move takes place?

These parents mean well. They are trying to spare their children pain. But in reality they are simply sparing themselves from dealing with something unpleasant. Children can handle the truth better than we think. I suspect parental dishonesty does far more harm than good. Eventually the child is going to figure out that Mom and Dad have been untruthful. And then the question comes: When *can* Mom and Dad's word be trusted?

Let me hasten to say that I do not think it is always necessary to tell children everything. If a beloved grandparent has terminal cancer, it isn't necessary to describe to a child the extent of suffering the loved one will experience. But don't tell the child that Grandma is going to be "just fine" in order to shield him from pain. What happens when he comes home from school and learns that Grandma is dead? Would it not have been better if he had been prepared for the imminent death?

The reward for honesty with our children is that they will learn that just as God is reliable, so are their parents. We can be trusted to give them the straight story. And as we help our children deal with reality, we will help them become mature human beings.

Remember Jesus' story about the self-righteous Pharisee and the humble tax collector:

> To those trusting in their own righteousness and looking down on the rest, He told this parable: "Two men went up to the temple to pray, the one a Pharisee and the other a tax collector. The Pharisee stood up and said this prayer to himself, 'God, I thank Thee that I am not like the rest of men — robbers, cheats, adulterers; or even like this tax collector. I fast twice a week; I pay tithes on everything I get.' But the tax collector, standing at a distance, would not even raise his eyes toward heaven, but struck his chest and said, 'God, be merciful to me, the sinner.' I tell you, it was he who went home forgiven, rather than the other; for whoever exalts himself will be

humbled, but he who humbles himself will be exalted" (Luke 18:9-14, Berkeley).

God has made it possible for us to be restored to a full and joyful relationship with Him when we are willing to be honest with Him and with ourselves. Until we have faced our own spiritual poverty, we are simply playing games. Until we are willing to be honest with our children, we are in no position to lead them.

Third, we must steer away from a rigid view of our human frailties. Constant emphasis on the bad things a child does distorts the teachings of Scripture. Yes, we are bad in and of ourselves. But we are not *all* bad for we have been made in the image and likeness of God, who is all good. And as Christians God sees us as good and worthwhile — even highly prized through Jesus Christ. Good self-esteem is built by having a right view of ourselves. Poor self-esteem results when we have a distorted view.

A friend tells about the nursery school her daughter attended while they were living in Scotland. The philosophy of the classroom aide seemed to center on teaching by intimidation and humiliation.

When Timmy acted up in class, the aide would announce within earshot of everyone, "What a horrrrible little boy you are. What a horrrrible little boy," she'd scold, rolling her Scottish r's dramatically.

When young Mary, who came from a severely disadvantaged home, turned in a messy paper, the aide held the paper up for everyone to see and declared, "What a terrrribly messy paper Mary has done. Shame on you, Mary."

Just as the aide's own distorted viewpoint destroyed the children's self-esteem, the view of sin we subscribe to is the one we will pass on to our children. And it is out of this context that a young child will begin to form his or her self-esteem.

What kind of self-esteem do you think young Timmy and Mary will develop if they are subjected to a constant diet of "shame on you" and "you are horrible"?

Every year during soccer season, I hear coaches who attempt to teach by intimidation and others who teach by emphasizing the positive in a realistic way. There are a few coaches who swear at the boys and deride them for missing the ball or who yell sarcastic comments like, "What are you doing out there, Tommy? Watching the birds fly over?" Under that kind of coaching, I have seen our boys become discouraged and want to quit. Badgering and intimidating do nothing to teach a boy how to play soccer.

And then I hear the coaches who holler instructions instead of sarcasm — instructions that help a boy do his best. When a boy tries to kick the ball and misses, he hears his coach say, "That's OK, Bobby. You'll get it next time." One season, after every game, I heard our boys' coach compliment each team member on something he had done right or well during the game. That kind of coaching helps a boy become a better team player.

The adult with low self-esteem constantly criticizes others in order to build himself up in his own eyes.

Each of us then is born into this world with a tendency toward sin. But along with our sin nature God has given us the freedom to choose to be different. And that leads us to the third factor that helps shape a child's life: freedom of choice.

5

FREE TO CHOOSE

We choose our joys and sorrows long before we experience them.

Kahlil Gibran

Mark is the third son of a black father and a white mother. During much of his growing-up years his father was absent from home. Money was scarce, his brothers were frequently in trouble with the law, and the positive male role model Mark needed was not there. Mark's two older brothers are currently serving prison sentences for murder.

Given Mark's overwhelming disadvantages, you would not be surprised if I told you that Mark has not amounted to much. However, just the opposite is true. From his earliest years this young man's life has been in direct contrast to his two older brothers.

When he graduated from high school, Mark, an excellent athlete, turned down a sports scholarship to a prominent university. He felt too much pressure would be placed on him to pursue athletics. He really wanted to concentrate on the academics.

At Easter one year, Mark gathered other college students who couldn't afford to go home for the holiday and fixed dinner for them.

Three brothers — raised in the same home under the same set of circumstances — yet Mark chose a constructive way of life. His brothers chose just the opposite.

Why?

You might remember the story of two brothers mentioned in the first book of the Bible. Their names were Cain and Abel. Two boys raised in the same home with the same set of parents, yet the choices they made were distinctly different. Abel was a good man who followed God. Cain only pretended to follow God and, when things didn't go his way, he killed his brother.

If environment is so important, how can two children raised in the same home with the same advantages and disadvantages turn out so differently.?

Why does an abused child from a broken, alcoholic home end up a productive member of society?

Why does a child raised in a "good Christian home" by loving parents, who taught him right from wrong, end up on drugs or in prison?

We have already noted the role that perception and our sin nature play in a child's growth and development. We come now to the third factor, the area of *freedom of choice*.

INSTINCT VERSUS FREE WILL

One remarkable difference between man and the animal world is the difference between instinct and free will. In the animal world, basic needs such as food, shelter, propagation, and rest are programmed into the animal. We call it instinct.

The kiwi bird does not have to make a conscious decision about what kind of nest it will build. It knows instinctively what is needed for survival and the protection of its young. Our family dog does not make a decision to eat less dog food this week so he can shed a few pounds. He just eats because he is hungry. But if the food is spoiled, he knows instinctively not to touch it.

Human beings are different. We do not operate on the basis of mere instinct. Every day our lives are filled with *conscious choices* about what we will eat, what we will wear, where we will go, what we will say and what we will do.

It is man — not animals — who was created in the image of God. And part of that image is the freedom to make choices.

WHY DO WE HAVE A FREE WILL?

Why do we have a free will? What's the point of it? Wouldn't it be a lot less complicated if God had simply made us robots, eternally programmed to do what is right? That's what it must have looked like in heaven when only God and the angels inhabited it. But after Satan's rebellion and Adam and Eve's disobedience, we mortals inherited both the sin nature and free will.

What is the point of having a free will? Surely it relates to our being made in the image of God. God is not a robot; neither are we. Robots do not have loving relationships. They only function — or malfunction. We humans are created in the image of God — a God who desires to have a loving relationship with us. That relationship, to be effective and satisfying, must be based on choice. We must make the conscious choice to love and serve God. He is not going to force us to love Him. But *He* has made the choice to love us whether we love Him or not. That is a powerful fact.

It is free will that allows our children to make both right and wrong choices.

IS SOCIETY TO BLAME?

For many decades we have been told that a person's environment is responsible for his behavior. We've heard it described as "Society is more to blame for the crime than the criminal." Or, "It's the parents' fault if their child turns out badly."

It was with that attitude that Dr. Stanton E. Samenow, a clinical psychologist and member of President Reagan's Task Force on Victims of Crime, began his work with delinquent adolescents.

> When I began this work, I believed that criminal behavior was a symptom of buried conflicts that had resulted from early traumas and deprivation of one sort or another. I thought that people who turned to crime were victims of a psychological disorder, an oppressive social environment, or both. From my work in Michigan with inner city youths, I saw crime as being almost a normal, if not excusable, reaction to the grinding poverty, instability, and despair that pervaded their lives. On the other hand, I thought that kids who were from more advantaged backgrounds had been scarred by bad parenting and led astray by peer pressure.[1]

With much reluctance and debate, Dr. Samenow discovered that he had to "unlearn nearly everything that I had learned in graduate school." After several years of studying and trying to help delinquent young people, Dr. Samenow was forced to conclude that other factors were at work in delinquent youth besides parental input. That something was freedom of choice. It became obvious to him that:

> Delinquent youngsters come from all social classes and from all kinds of homes. . . . Each of them thinks and acts differently from responsible members of his own family. At an early age, each begins making a series of choices to live a life that he considers exciting, a life in which he is determined to do whatever he wants, a life in which he ignores restraints and eventually turns against his family and scoffs at those who live responsible lives. Each complains about unfair treatment and is perceived by others as a hapless victim of his parents' pathology or a malfunctioning family unit. But this is not the case. The theories that purport to explain delinquency by blam-

ing parents are misleading and potentially harmful. Such youngsters *choose* the life they want.

MAKING CHOICES: A LIFELONG OCCUPATION

As soon as our children are old enough to think and act for themselves, freedom of choice is at work.

How many times have you said, "I told you not to hit your sister with the truck, Sammy?" As you take the truck from your three-year-old, you're still ranting, "Why did you do it again?"

He may tell you that he forgot, or that it's all his sister's fault because she hit him first. But the truth of the matter is, Sammy hit his sister with the truck because he wanted to. He *chose* to become the aggressor.

Why did your teenager break her curfew and come home forty-five minutes late? Did you fail to tell her what time to be home? No, she made a *conscious choice* to adhere to peer pressure, rather than obey her parents.

The Old Testament is full of stories of those who chose to do evil or to do good, despite their home environment and their instruction regarding right and wrong. Take for example the family of Hezekiah, one of the kings of Israel, whose progenitors see-sawed back and forth in their choice of lifestyle.

Hezekiah was one of the best kings Israel ever had. 2 Kings 18:3 says, "And he did what was right in the eyes of the LORD, according to all that David his father had done" (RSV).

His son Manasseh was raised in a God-fearing family, but when he became king, he chose evil. "And he did what was evil in the sight of the LORD, according to the abominable practices of the nations whom the LORD drove out before the people of Israel" (2 Kings 21:2, RSV).

Manasseh's son Amon was an evil ruler. But when Amon's son Josiah took over the kingdom, he "did what was right in the eyes of the LORD, and walked in all the way of David his father, and he did not turn aside to the right hand or to the left" (2 Kings 22:2, RSV).

Knofel Station writes in *Bible Keys for Today's Family:*

> Maturing children is not like manufacturing automobiles. We can't just stamp out the design *we* want. After all the stuff we have poured into them, our children will eventually make their own choices about priorities, values, life-styles, and goals. Don't get me wrong. What we model is important, but it doesn't fully guarantee the outcome of our kids. Kids reach their adult years without any good housekeeping warranty.
>
> Some of our kids will become better than we; some will become worse; none will become clones.[3]

PARENTS DON'T MAKE CRIMINALS

At one time or another, most children lie, steal, cheat or make other wrong choices. It's a part of growing up and growing out of bad behavior which is our tendency by nature. However, the delinquent child establishes an early pattern of bad behavior and no matter how loving or how abusive his parents may be, he continues to pursue this pattern.

Are the parents responsible for this pattern of behavior? Dr. Samenow — and I — think not.

> Few parents remain indifferent or give up. They do what they can — spend more time with the child, enroll him in a different school, support his joining organized sports and clubs, send him to a counselor, seek counseling themselves. In grasping at possible solutions, the soul-searching goes on. Mothers and fathers blame themselves, each other, and people and events outside the family. They devour psychologically oriented books and then identify themselves as the causes of their child's delinquency. Some parents seek therapy.
>
> There comes a time when parents of such a child have to face the fact that they are powerless to change the course of events.[4]

WHAT'S A PARENT TO DO?

Is all this terribly frustrating? Do you believe that no matter what you do as a parent, your kids are liable to blow everything?

Remember, when we talk about delinquent children we are talking about a minority group. *Most* kids are not juvenile delinquents. *Most* kids do not make serious life-changing mistakes. *Most* kids turn out to be decent, law-abiding citizens.

Fortunately, there is a positive side to the aspect of freedom of choice as well as a negative. Our children are also free to make *right* choices.

We watch with pride the child who resists the temptation to cheat on a history test, even if it means getting a low grade. We're proud of the child who says no to drugs. The reward of doing what is right is an added incentive for the children who continue to make right choices.

Although most children turn out well, we as parents suffer over the few who make wrong choices. They also suffer. God knows just how we feel. He grieves over each of us when *we* choose our own way instead of His. He lamented over the sins of Israel, crying, "What more could I have done?" and "Why did my vineyard give me wild grapes instead of sweet?" (Isaiah 5:4, TLB).

At times we are just as stubborn as the children of Israel or our own wayward children. Perhaps we are most stubborn in wanting them to turn out "perfect" — free of the trials and tribulations that can make them stronger Christians.

God grieves with us over our children's wrong choices. But unless we have truly wronged our children in some way, He does not judge *us* for their actions. He says so quite clearly in Ezekiel 18:1-5, 9-10, 13b, 20:

> Then the LORD's message came to me again.
> "Why do people use this proverb about the land of Israel: The children are punished for their fathers' sins? As I live, says the LORD God, you will not use this

proverb any more in Israel, for all souls are mine to judge — fathers and sons alike — and my rule is this: It is for man's own sins that he will die.

"But if a man is just and does what is lawful and right . . . and obeys my laws — that man is just, says the LORD, and he shall surely live.

"But if that man has a son who is a robber or murderer and who fulfills none of his responsibilities . . . shall that man live? No! He shall surely die, and it is his own fault . . .

"The one who sins is the one who dies. The son shall not be punished for his father's sins, nor the father for his son's. The righteous person will be rewarded for his own goodness and the wicked person for his wickedness" (TLB).

In His patient, compassionate way God the Father never gives up on us. Sometimes He knows that the only way we will learn is to make mistakes. When we have had enough of our own way and when we come to Him ready to confess our need of *His* direction in our lives, He stands ready to forgive and to forget. We do not find God wallowing in guilt for some imagined failure on His part. Instead, He is eager to help us turn negatives into positives and get on with the business of living.

The choices set before our children are precisely those which God sets before all of us:

See, I have set before you this day life and good, death and evil. If you obey the commandments of the LORD your God which I command you this day, by loving the LORD your God, by walking in his ways, and by keeping his commandments and his statutes and his ordinances, then you shall live and multiply, and the LORD your God will bless you in the land which you are entering to take possession of it. But if your heart turns away, and you will not hear, but are drawn away to worship other gods and serve them, I declare to you this day, that you shall perish; you shall not live long in the land which you are going over the Jordan to enter and possess. I call heaven and earth to witness against you this day, that I have set before you life and death, blessing and curse; therefore choose life, that you and your descendants may live, loving the LORD your God, obeying his voice, and cleaving to him; for that means life to you and length of days, that you may dwell in the land which the LORD swore to your fathers, to Abraham, to Isaac, and to Jacob, to give them (Deuteronomy 30:15-20, RSV).

In the same way that God instructs us in our choices and their consequences, even so we instruct our children. But we cannot program their choices. What we *can* do is trust God to take even the bad choices in both our lives and theirs and use them to bring us closer to Him.

6

CONFRONTING THE GHOSTS OF THE PAST

[Forgiving] is love's unexpected revolution against unfair pain and it alone offers strong hope for healing the hurts we so unfairly feel.
           Lewis Smedes
           Forgive and Forget

A missionary friend tells of the time he had to leave his family in an Asian country and return to the States. He had a dream one night that all five of his children were lined up in front of him, but there was an invisible wall separating him from his oldest son. None of the warmth he felt for the other four children was flowing to this one son.

When he woke up he was deeply troubled and went downstairs to have tea with a counselor friend. He shared his dream with his friend. Knowing that the counselor had had training in interpreting dreams, he asked him what the dream meant. His friend answered with five simple words: "Tell me about your father."

His words struck the missionary to the very heart. He broke down and fled to his room utterly devastated. There he poured out his heart to God asking forgiveness for the anger and bitterness toward his own father which had built up over the years. When he returned to his family, the wall between him and his oldest son was gone.

"If you have unresolved conflicts with a parent," my friend says, "expect those conflicts to arise between you and your first-born child who is the same sex as your parent."

Some of our guilt and conflict regarding our children have their roots in unresolved conflicts with our own parents. We are not perfect parents and neither were our parents. If you were a child who suffered serious traumas at the hands of your parents — neglect, abuse or an extremely unstable home life — your feelings of anger are perfectly normal. But if left unresolved, that anger will compound until it affects every area of your life. It will most assuredly affect your relationship with your own children.

"My mother came from a small town in Puerto Rico," says Rosalita, a lovely dark-eyed mother of three. "As the oldest of eleven children, it was mother's job to help care for her younger brothers and sisters. My mother was never mothered. Instead, she had to *be a mother* from the time her second sibling was born."

When Rosalita's mother grew up and had a family of her own, she followed the same pattern. "Even though there were only two of us and my brother was only fifteen months younger than I," Rosalita says, "my mother expected me to take care of him. If my brother did something wrong, it was my fault. I wasn't a good enough *mother*. And my mother would beat me for what my brother did wrong. Afterwards she would suffer great remorse and wouldn't speak to me for three or four hours. For a time after that she would still act cold toward me. That coldness was more devastating for me than the beating."

There is a sadness in Rosalita's eyes when she adds, "Would you believe the same pattern showed up when I became a foster parent? I had three foster children at the time — all boys — and I complained to my husband that I needed help with the kids. He asked, 'What do you need — a maid, a housekeeper, or what?' Without thinking, I replied, *'I need a daughter.'* "

In *Making Peace With Your Parents,* psychiatrist Harold H. Bloomfield suggests that as parents we may overcompensate with our own children for what our parents did or did not do for us. For example, if our parents were strict and moralistic, we may swing to the opposite extreme and allow our children to run their own lives as they see fit. Or we may resent the freedom our children have because we never had much as children. Worse yet, we may discover ourselves doing to our children the same things our parents did to us. Parents who experienced violence at the hands of their own parents often repeat that pattern with their own children.

That was Rosalita's experience. Beatings were common when she was growing up. When her own son was born, the pattern almost repeated itself.

"One day I was sitting in a chair sewing," she recalls, "and my very young son was playing across the room. He wasn't doing anything wrong at all. It was a very peaceful scene. But suddenly I was struck with the awful urge to hit him. I was shocked at the depth of my feeling when the child was being so good!

"Fortunately," Rosalita says, "I had enough presence of mind and self-discipline not to hit him. I picked him up, put him in his room and closed the door. Then I called my husband and a friend who came right home to me. I told them what had happened. It was at that point I knew I had to begin therapy. Only after my counseling did I understand why I had had such an urge to hit my son. It was because I had never been mothered. I had never enjoyed the good home environment he was enjoying and I was jealous."

Dr. Bloomfield tells about a lawyer he calls Roger who married for the first time at the age of forty. Roger's wife Eileen had two teenage sons by a previous marriage and from the very beginning, as Roger describes it, "they did everything in their power to make life difficult for me." When he laid down the law regarding their noisy friends, their messy rooms, or whatever, "those brats would go crying to their mother." As so often happens, soon the battles between the step-father and his step-sons became a battle between Roger and his wife. Dr. Bloomfield writes:

> When Roger and I began to explore his memories of childhood, similarities to his present situation appeared. Just as Roger had always felt that his younger brothers "stole" his mother's affection away from him, so did he resent the competition for Eileen's affection. Just as Roger had rebelled against his father's angry outbursts about his "messy room," so was Roger becoming dictatorial about the boys' rooms. As Roger lamented, "For years I avoided getting married and starting a family because I couldn't imagine being a parent. When I wound up playing the role of 'Dad' to Eileen's kids, I swore I'd do it right. Now it looks as though I'm no better than my old man."[1]

In *Finding Our Fathers,* Dr. Samuel Osherson notes another area of potential conflict which can occur between a father and his children if the father has distorted views of his own father and the masculine role. The traditional male role has been that of the breadwinner who provides for his family, but who is distant from his children either physically or emotionally or both. The mother, on the other hand, is the nurturer, the helper, the one who takes care of her children's emotional needs and also her husband's. A growing boy, attempting to separate from his mother and become like his father, is often embarrassed by the need he feels to be nurtured and taken care of by his parent. Traditionally men have not learned nurturing and intimacy from their own fathers, hence, they equate such characteristics as feminine.

Dr. Osherson observes that:

> ... those of us who have grown up during the decades in which the women's movement became a powerful force are experiencing social changes of epic proportions: the clear and direct movement of women into positions of greater power and equality in the workplace and the movement of men into family life . . .
>
> Today, when a wife goes to work, when a baby arrives, or when the family reorganizes upon the departure of children to college, the man is less able to turn to trad-

itional sex roles and expectations. He is often put back in touch with feelings of helplessness and powerlessness that he did not entirely master as a child and is caught by surprise, often feeling a pain he can't really understand . . .

The key to the unfinished business of manhood is unraveling and letting go of our distorted and painful misidentifications with our fathers.[2]

HOW TO GET RID OF RESENTMENTS

What was your childhood experience? Do you carry the scars of physical or mental abuse? Have you struggled with the desire to know more fully a distant parent?

Is it possible to forgive your parents for the real or imagined wrongs they committed against you? Yes, it is. And forgiving them is essential to your own growth and maturity as a person and as a parent. Resentment stifles growth and causes us to wither and die. Forgiveness frees us to become all God wants us to be. Do you think the hurts are too deep or the scars too thick to ever forgive your parents for what they did to you? Please keep reading. God in you can do the impossible.

Listed below are several steps you can take to rid yourself of resentments and to help you forgive your parents for whatever wrongs they committed against you. The first five are suggested by Dr. Bloomfield.

1. *Make a list of all the resentments you hold toward your parents.* Be specific and include details:

- I resent you for never complimenting me on anything I do well.
- I resent you for spanking me in front of my friends when I was ten.
- I resent you for always blaming me when things go wrong.

Make your list as long as you wish but *do not show it to your parents.* The purpose of the list is to help you release the resentments that have been pent up inside you for so long.

2. *Imagine your parent listening to and accepting you.*

As a small child you were unable to speak up for yourself and tell your parents when they did something you resented. But since you are an adult now, you no longer need to feel victimized.

Find a quiet spot where you will not be interrupted and picture in your mind's eye your parent listening to you attentively, accepting what you have to say and acknowledging the pain you feel. Then read your list of resentments, allowing yourself to scream out loud or cry if it helps you release those angry, pent-up feelings. Regardless of how your parent would actually respond, picture him or her accepting and comforting you. This experience may be emotionally draining, but it is important.

3. *Write a letter to your parent expressing all the feelings that have long been suppressed.* It may take you a day or two to complete it. Write out all your anger and hurts in detail. *Do not send the letter.* While this exercise will be helpful for you, it would play havoc if you actually sent it to your parent!

4. To further the healing process, *find a friend, spouse, or sibling whom you trust and ask the person to sit and listen to you read your list of resentments.* This person should *not* be your parent. The only words this person is allowed to say are "OK," "Tell me more" or "I got it." When you are finished thank your friend for his support in helping you work toward healing.

5. *Make an "I forgive you" list to help uncover the hidden blocks to forgiveness.* No matter how good your intentions, you will find yourself resisting actually forgiving your parent. Your list should look something like this:

Dear Mom:

I forgive you.	No I don't. Not really.
I forgive you.	But I'm still afraid of you,
I forgive you.	Except when you try to manipulate me.
I forgive you.	Only because you make me feel guilty.
I forgive you.	I'd like to, anyway.
I forgive you.	It's not easy after your phone calls.
I forgive you.	But I wish you could see me for who

	I am and not who you want me to be.
	If you weren't trying to live through
	me I could relax more around you.
I forgive you.	Maybe. I don't know.
I forgive you.	This feels strange. Almost numb.
I forgive you.	This is taking too long.
I forgive you.	I wish you'd just know that I love you.
I forgive you.	I care, but it's hard to show you.
I forgive you.	If only I could be sure I was safe to
	be myself around you.
I forgive you.	(nothing)
I forgive you.	(nothing)
I forgive you.	(nothing)[3]

6. *Another method, which you may find helpful if your parent is dead, is to visit your parent's grave.* Sit down beside the grave and talk to your parent, pouring out your anger, hurt and resentments. Then tell your parent that you forgive him or her, even though the person is not there to hear you.

7. *Think of something you did (maybe only one thing) that your parent enjoyed.* Dr. Osherson suggests that "creative solutions such as the arts, music, crafts, which allow the exploration of the self," may help bring healing. He offers the following example:

> One man in a childless marriage, who felt his father left him emotionally at age five, remembered as an adult how much he and his father both loved music. He plays the piano as a hobby today, but recently he realized how much hidden love lay secretly in their shared love of the instrument. "My involvement in music seemed to express a repressed part in himself . . . He especially liked to walk around in the backyard in the summer listening to the sounds of my piano practicing coming through the back windows." This man had completely forgotten for twenty years the pleasure his father took in the son's talent; he spoke now of imagining his father listening happily at the window when he plays the piano, transforming his image of father as a demanding, withdrawn presence into a satisfied, supportive one.[4]

8. *Ask God to heal your hurts and help you forgive*

your parents. God is the great Healer and He wants you to be whole. He does not want to see the same problems perpetuated from one generation to another. He has promised that when you call, He will answer.

One thing that can help you forgive your parents is to realize that you are capable of the same sins as theirs. When I heard ministers say that we are all capable of each and every sin, it used to confuse me. I would think of the most awful sin imaginable and then think, "But I would never do that." At that point in my life, I probably wouldn't have.

Then someone explained it to me this way: "Given the same set of circumstances and the same background of experiences as the person who committed the crime or sin, we would probably do the same thing." It is much easier to forgive when we understand our own vulnerability.

In *Forgive and Forget,* Lewis Smedes writes:

> When I am counseling a man who admits to having hurt someone he loved, I put myself in his place and wonder whether I would have done all that much better than he did. And I know in my heart that I may well have done no better.
>
> I do not think I am being morbid. I think that I am reminding myself that much of my apparent virtue is nothing but good luck and the grace of God. Put me in other circumstances, where to be honest or courageous requires a very high price, and I could not guarantee anyone that I would be a hero.[5]

Earlier in the book Dr. Smedes poses the question: Why forgive? Why should people be allowed to cut us down and hurt us to the very depths of our souls — and get away with it? Do they really have a right to expect us to just forgive them as if nothing had ever happened? Why forgive? he asks.

> And we shall answer: because forgiving is the *only* way we have to a better fairness in our unfair world; it is love's unexpected revolution against unfair pain and it

alone offers strong hope for healing the hurts we so unfairly feel.[6]

This chapter barely scratches the surface of resolving conflicts with our parents. If this is an area of concern for you, I would urge you to read the following books:

Howard M. Halpern, *Cutting Loose: An Adult Guide to Coming to Terms with Your Parents* (Bantam Books).

Samuel Osherson, *Finding Our Fathers, The Unfinished Business of Manhood* (The Free Press).

Lewis B. Smedes, *Forgive and Forget, Healing the Hurts We Don't Deserve* (Harper & Row).

Harold H. Bloomfield, *Making Peace with Your Parents* (Random House).

H. Norman Wright, *Making Peace with Your Past* (Fleming H. Revell).

7

COUNTERING NEGATIVE THOUGHTS

For Thou causest my lamp to shine; the LORD, my God, illumines my darkness. For by Thee I can attack a troop, and by my God I can leap a wall.
                              Psalm 18:28,29, Berkeley

When Ron and Denise got married, it wasn't exactly a marriage made in heaven. On the outside, however, it looked reasonably stable. Denise's mother Gwen was happy that her daughter had found someone to marry. It had not been easy raising Denise as a single parent, but Gwen was satisfied that she had done the best she could.

In a couple of years Ron and Denise had a baby girl. Ten months later they discovered that she was mildly retarded. From then on, things were never the same. When their daughter was nine, Ron decided he no longer wanted to be married to Denise, nor did he want to be the father of a retarded child. He split and has no contact whatsoever with his daughter.

Things were rough. Denise tried to be a good mother, but eventually the strain caught up with her. She refused to join any kind of support group for parents of retarded children. Instead she finally placed her daughter in a foster home and called it quits.

Her mother Gwen was devastated. Such irresponsibility was beyond her comprehension. The horror of the irreparable harm being done to her granddaughter was more than Gwen could bear.

"I cried," Gwen says, "until my eyes dried out. I went to the doctor and he gave me a bottle of liquid to put in my eyes. I had literally run out of tears. I told him I never thought I'd have to buy tears."

For over a year Gwen tried in vain to help Denise work things out. But Denise wanted help from no one, especially her mother. She wanted to be free of the responsibility of a retarded child and to get on with her life. Nothing Gwen said or did made any difference.

"I never thought I raised a daughter to be like this," Gwen admitted, guilt edging her voice.

"You didn't, Gwen," I replied. "You set just the opposite example for her. You raised Denise alone and even when it was tough you didn't give up on her."

"No, I didn't," Gwen agreed, common sense trying to push aside the guilt, "I know I didn't raise her to be like this. I knew when I got pregnant with her that my marriage wasn't going to last. I could have stopped the pregnancy but I chose not to. I wanted to have my child. It was never easy but I didn't give up. But today's kids aren't like that."

Intellectually, Gwen knew that she wasn't to blame for what Denise did. But the battle wasn't over yet, was it? There were still two accusers who could continue to try and make Gwen feel guilty. Those two accusers were (1) her inner thoughts and (2) other people.

Is it possible to face our accusers head on and end the guilt? Yes, indeed. Remember, it is not *God* who is accusing us. He wants us to be at peace — and He will help us handle our accusers.

Let's begin by discovering some ways that we can deal with our inner thoughts.

GUILT AND SELF-ESTEEM

We need to be aware that there is a high correlation between guilt and self-esteem. When we feel guilty, we do not feel like we have much worth. By the same token, when we do not feel we have much self-worth, it is easy for us to feel responsible for other people's problems. If our past experiences cause constant feelings of inferiority, it is harder to shake off our accusers.

For the purposes of this chapter, I would like us to take a look at three factors that contribute to our self-esteem. Understanding each of them can help us change a negative self-image into a positive one. In the process, we will also rid ourselves of a load of guilt.

1. *Parental approval.* Our first feelings of self-worth form when we are very small children; these feelings continue to develop for many years. If our parents approve, accept and praise us for what we do right as well as correct us when we do wrong, we usually develop a healthy self-esteem. But if our parents constantly criticize us and belittle our efforts, we grow up feeling we have little worth. In his book *Self Esteem,* Cecil Osborne says:

> Children who are constantly criticized come to believe that they are unlovable. If they do not receive love in a form they can accept, they feel, "I must be worthless, or they would love me, care for me, hold me." Holding is a physical manifestation of caring. Children who receive little or no touching inevitably feel rejected and thus unworthy: "If I am worthless, then I am not worthy of success." The battered children — and there are millions of them — usually grow up with monumental feelings of unworthiness and vague, diffused senses of shame or guilt.
>
> Though it is seldom dealt with, the following emotions all have a common denominator:
>
> | Failure | Shame | Rejection | Inadequacy |
> |---|---|---|---|
> | Guilt | Unworthiness | Inferiority | |
>
> One who as a child *felt* loved and affirmed seldom experiences any of those seven manifestations of weak self-esteem; for as psychiatrist Karl Menninger has said, "Love is the medicine for the healing of the world."[1]

2. *The Church.* A second source for our self-esteem comes from the church in which we were raised. Some churches are loving, affirming centers for spiritual growth. Other churches concentrate on the negatives of the Christian life — what unworthy sinners we are and the lists of do's and don'ts. The person with low self-worth may feed on these negatives because it confirms what the person already "knows" about himself or herself: "I am unworthy."

Take Catherine for example. When Catherine became a Christian, she quickly accepted the rather strict expectations of her church. She stopped going to movies and dances and removed her make-up. Her church said these things were wrong.

When you get to know Catherine, however, you discover that the "thou shalt nots" in her life are as much an expression of her feelings of inferiority as they are of the teachings of her church. If she has such little worth, why should she use make-up to make herself look more attractive? If her church is more qualified to interpret Scripture, then why should she question any of its mandates?

In the book *Your Better Self,* Anthony A. Hoekema writes:

> In Reformed or Calvinistic circles, we often have a self-image that over-accentuates the negative. We tend to see ourselves through the purple-colored glasses of our depravity. We have been writing of our continuing sinfulness in capital letters and of our newness in Christ in very small letters. We tend to believe in total depravity so strongly that we think we have to practice it, while we hardly dare to believe in our newness.
>
> It is, however, not only among Calvinists that this morbid preoccupation with sin and depravity is found . . . When properly understood and taken in its totality, the New Testament repudiates this kind of negative self-image. For what the New Testament writers emphasize is that the Christian is a *new creature* — who, to be sure, continues to struggle against sin during this life, but does so as one who is more than a conqueror through Christ.[2]

Do you dread taking communion at church because you are afraid there is unconfessed sin in your life and you are eating and drinking damnation to your soul? Or, do you ask God to reveal any hidden sin and when none becomes evident, can you celebrate Christ's death in joy and thankfulness for what He has done for you?

The over-emphasis on our sinful nature and our unworthiness completely overlooks the fact that we are made in the image of God and that we are to live joyfully and positively as His beloved children. As the saying goes, "God doesn't make junk." When we allow feelings of guilt to rule our lives, we are living outside His will and plan for our lives. This continually erodes our self-esteem. We cannot think of anything in particular we did wrong, but because we are sinners we must have done something!

As Hoekema puts it:

> Nothing contributes more to a negative self-image than feelings of guilt. When people are obsessed by guilt feelings, they despise themselves, feel utterly worthless, and are likely to plunge into the depths of depression.[3]

What a self-defeating way to live!

3. *The Teachings of Scripture.* It would seem rather obvious to suggest that we should derive our feelings of self-worth from Scripture. But all too often, instead of finding out what the Bible says, we rely on someone else's interpretation of Scripture. Sometimes that interpretation is negative rather than positive. In fact, what it should be is *realistic.*

Paul tells us in Romans 12:3, "For through the grace that is granted me I warn each one among you not to value himself more highly than he should, but to think soberly as God has measured out to each his portion of faith" (Berkeley).

Anthony Hoekema comments:

> To think more highly of ourselves than we ought to think is pride. To think less highly of ourselves than we ought to think is false modesty. To think soberly ("with

sober judgment") about ourselves is to think realistically, to take stock of the talents and abilities God has given us, and to make an honest appraisal of ourselves.[4]

Our feelings of self-worth carry over into all areas of our lives including our roles as parents. Do we set rules for our children and stick to them? Or do we constantly wonder if we have done the right thing and change the rules when our child is unhappy about them?

Do we put ourselves down in front of our spouse and our children? It is very hard to respect a person who does not respect himself or herself.

Do we criticize and blame our spouse or our children when things go wrong, even when we are the ones who are at fault? Are we tearing other people down in order to build ourselves up in our own eyes? Or do we quickly admit when we have done something wrong, ask forgiveness, and put the matter behind us?

What does the Bible say about our self-worth? Study these verses compiled in Jan Congo's book, *Finding Inner Security*. We find our true self-worth only when we are rightly connected to God through Jesus Christ. These truths from Scripture show us just how much God thinks of us.

> He is the loving, concerned Father who is interested in the intimate details of our lives (Matthew 6:25-34).
>
> He is the Father who never gives up on us (Luke 15:3-32).
>
> He is the God who sent His Son to die for us though we were undeserving (Romans 5:8).
>
> He stands with us in the good and bad circumstances (Hebrews 13:5).
>
> He died to heal sickness, pain and our grief (Isaiah 53:3-6).

He has broken the power of death (Luke 24:6-7).

He gives all races and sexes equal status (Galatians 3:28).

He is available to us through prayer (John 14:13-14).

He is aware of our needs (Isaiah 65:24).

He has created us for an eternal relationship with him (John 3:16).

He values us (Luke 7:28).

He doesn't condemn us (Romans 8:1).

God values and causes our growth (1 Corinthians 3:7).

He comforts us (2 Corinthians 1:3-5).

He strengthens us through His Spirit (Ephesians 3:16).

He cleanses us (Hebrews 10;17-22).

He is for us (Romans 8:31).

He is always available to us (Romans 8:38-39).

He is the God of hope (Romans 15:13).

He provides a way to escape temptations (1 Corinthians 10:13).

He is at work in us (Philippians 2:13).

He helps us in temptation (Hebrews 2:17-18).

He wants us to be free (Galatians 5:1).

He is the final Lord of History (Revelation 1:8).[5]

Now I ask you: Would God be *that* concerned about you if you were a worthless human being?

By loving us with unconditional love, God has declared us to be worthy individuals. Whether we accept Him or reject Him, He goes on loving us. When we sin, He does not like the sin, but He does not stop loving us. When we repent, He accepts us with open arms and remembers our sin no more.

Who but a loving God, who created us, could hold us in such high esteem? Therefore, what right do we have to hold ourselves in low esteem?

COUNTERING NEGATIVE THOUGHTS

There are three basic kinds of thoughts that enter our minds.

There are *neutral or factual thoughts:* "The sun is shining." Neutral or factual thoughts are non-judgmental. They simply state the way something is.

There are *positive thoughts:* "It's going to be sunny all day and I love the warmth of the sun!" Positive thoughts are based on a feeling that all is well with the world or is going to be well.

And there are *negative thoughts:* "I'll bet it's going to be 100 degrees today and I hate the heat!" Both positive and negative thoughts are subjective in nature. They are based on attitude, conditioning, and a host of other variables.

Some people are basically positive. They generally see the silver lining in the storm clouds. Other people are basically negative. They are the first to point out the negatives in any situation. Many of us are somewhere in the middle, between these two opposites.

Obviously, positive thoughts are more beneficial than negative ones. Both of them have their extremes, however. Positive thoughts that are not based on a realistic appraisal of life lead to the Pollyanna approach — never facing up to life's problems. Negative thoughts, in the extreme, lead to depression.

The Bible says, "A cheerful heart makes a good cure, but a broken spirit makes the bones dry up" (Proverbs 17:22, Berkeley). Positive thoughts can help eliminate the negative guilt-enforcing thoughts. But often we allow the negative thoughts to overrule. Even though we have confessed our wrongdoing to God and been forgiven, or acknowledged false guilt for what it is, our inner thoughts may still try to condemn us.

"You should have tried harder."

"You can excuse yourself all you want. But you know if you had been there, your son's accident would never have happened."

"Don't try to kid yourself. You're to blame and you know it."

Just as a plant will not grow if it is trampled on continuously, even so you cannot grow emotionally strong if you are crushed with negative thoughts. Plants need the warmth of the sun, the coolness of the earth and the dampness of a spring rain in order to grow, blossom and bloom. Even so, you need positive reinforcement for what you know to be true — that you were never to blame in the first place or that you have been forgiven for whatever wrong you did commit.

For every negative thought, there is a positive counterpart. In all likelihood, it is the positive thought that is the correct one. Whenever you are tempted to blame yourself again, counter those thoughts with positive ones.

Here is a list of negative thoughts. Opposite each one write how you would counter it with a positive thought.

Negative Accusation	**Positive Reinforcement**
My son wouldn't be on drugs if I had been a better parent.	
Maybe if I'd done a better job talking about sex, my	

daughter wouldn't be pregnant.

Our son's marriage would never have ended like this if we had been better models as parents.

If I hadn't gone back to work, my daughter would probably have better grades.

Our child would never have been molested if we hadn't let him spend the night with his uncle.

I should never have let my son use the car. It's my fault he had that accident and was injured.

I should never have left my son alone in the house. If I had stayed home with him, he would never have committed suicide.

Somehow, we failed our daughter spiritually and now she's joined a cult. We should have forced her to go to church with us whether she wanted to or not.

Now compare your answers with the ones listed below.

Negative Accusation
My son wouldn't be on drugs if I had been a better parent.

Positive Reinforcement
He's getting good treatment and it looks like he's going to be OK.

Maybe if I'd done a better job talking about sex, my daughter wouldn't be pregnant.	I talked about sex as openly as I could with her. Now we need to focus on helping her make the right decision for the future.
Our son's marriage would never have ended like this if we had been better models as parents.	We have a good marriage. Sure we fight now and then but it doesn't last long and we always resolve the matter.
If I hadn't gone back to work, my daughter would have better grades.	Math has always been a problem for her. Now, we can finally afford the tutor she's been needing.
Our child would never have been molested if we hadn't let him spend the night with his uncle.	We had no reason to suspect his uncle of being anything but a loving, caring person. We have started counseling to help our child.
I should never have let my son use the car. It's my fault he had that accident and was injured.	He's got to learn responsibility. The accident seems to be making him act more maturely.
I should never have left my son alone in the house. If I had stayed home with him he would never have committed suicide.	I know now that he had been planning this for weeks. I am grateful that he knew I loved him.
Somehow, we failed our daughter spiritually and now she's joined a cult. We should have forced her to go to church with	She turned off to the church years ago. Forcing her to attend would have only made her more rebellious.

us whether she wanted to
or not.

USING POSITIVE IMAGERY

Imagination is a powerful God-given tool which can be used to find freedom from guilt. In his counseling practice, Norm Wright uses this technique of positive imagery to help people change the way they feel about themselves. I urge you to read his book, *Making Peace With Your Past* (Fleming H. Revell). One chapter is devoted to the use of imagery. He tells his counselees:

> "Sit back in your chair and close your eyes. Visualize a large blackboard with a mass of meaningless words and phrases written on it. As you look more closely this mass of words begins to spell out the acts or behaviors for which you do not feel forgiven. They now stand out clearly and boldly among the other words and phrases.
>
> "Now visualize Jesus Christ standing at the board. He is sweeping a damp sponge across that blackboard, wiping it clean. He keeps on until it is so clean that something fresh and new and meaningful can be written on it. God is erasing your past sin and failures so you can start again.
>
> "Now visualize Jesus beckoning you to come to the blackboard. He asks you to place your hand in His, and He says, 'I want you to see that the board has really been wiped clean. Feel My hand cleaning the board and believe that it is becoming clean and new again.' You feel His hand cleaning the board, and now it begins to dawn on you: Jesus is actually doing this for you.
>
> "Then visualize Jesus turning to you, placing His hand on your shoulder, and saying, 'You are forgiven. Experience my forgiveness as a part of your life. Live your life as a forgiven person.' By this action He is also telling you to forgive yourself, for there is no need to keep count of the errors on the blackboard. They no longer exist. It is as though someone hit the erase button on the calculator."

You may need to run this picture and sequence through your mind again and again until, through imaging, you experience the acceptance and forgiveness that are yours.[6]

In addition to countering our negative thoughts with positive ones, we also need to defuse the negative comments of others. That is the subject of the next chapter.

8

COPING WITH YOUR ACCUSERS

The tongue of the wise makes knowledge attractive, but the mouth of fools gushes forth with folly.
Proverbs 15:2, Berkeley

In chapter 6 I told you about Rosalita's early experience as a parent as she tried to avoid duplicating the violence she experienced as a child. But there is a darker side to her story which illustrates profoundly the false guilt that other people can dump on us.

When Rosalita was eight years old, her mother's boyfriend began molesting her. This horrifying experience lasted for four and a half years. At one point, Rosalita's aunt asked her what was going on. With someone finally ready to listen to the turmoil going on inside her, Rosalita told her aunt about the relationship.

"Don't let it happen again," her aunt warned her, as though the situation were all Rosalita's fault. "You can't tell anyone, you know, because if your father finds out, he will kill the man and it will be all your fault."

Her aunt was right. Her father would have killed the man, so the secret was once again locked inside the troubled girl.

Many years later, when her father did find out, he told Rosalita she should have told him at the time it was happening. Since she didn't tell him, she must have liked it, so she shouldn't be talking about it now.

Here was a young girl caught in the middle between her accusers, feeling that somehow, in some way utterly beyond her comprehension, a man's depravity must be her fault.

Ted's story, on the other hand, is quite different. Both he and the church he pastored were responsible for his feelings of guilt. When Ted's adult son became involved in drugs, Ted felt responsible. Believing firmly in the Bible and his church's admonition that a man who couldn't control his own family had no business running a church, Ted left the ministry and pursued secular work. He did not return to the ministry until his son got his act together several years later.

The world is full of people who are quick to blame us when things go wrong. When the situation is indeed our fault, the accusations may be justified. But all too often our accusers are in error or they misinterpret Scripture. Nevertheless, their accusations cut us to the quick.

How do you confront your accusers? Is there a Christian way to deal with the irresponsible judgmental comments of others? For a moment, let's identify our accusers and then look at some ways we can deal with them.

IDENTIFYING OUR ACCUSERS

Our kids. Our children may be the first to level an accusation at us. The very immaturity that got them into trouble also spurs them to put the blame on someone else. We, their loving parents, are first in line.

"Why did you let me take the car to the ballgame? If you'd let me go with my friends I would never have run into that other car."

"It's your fault I got an F in history, Dad. I have to spend so much time doing *your* work (washing the car, mowing the lawn, whatever); I don't have time to study."

In most situations it should be easy to spot who is actually to blame. If it's partly your fault, you can share the blame. But if you accept the blame for what your child did wrong, you are merely keeping him immature and irresponsible. Nobody needs a doormat for a parent.

Other family members. Those closest to us may be the quickest to come to our aid. They may also be the first to take us to task. Their very closeness may prevent them from looking objectively at the situation. Or perhaps they have an ax to grind already: "It's your fault. I never really approved of my daughter marrying you in the first place."

Witless wonders. There are some muddleheads who make it a policy never to think before they speak. They are famous for blunt, thoughtless and obnoxious statements. You know the kind: "I can't believe your daughter actually had an abortion. What on earth did you do to drive her to that?" Your best answer is silence. Why give your accuser ammunition?

People seeking answers. There are people who desperately need an answer as to why bad things happen. Perhaps their need for an answer is based on fear: "Could the same thing happen to me?"

When what I considered to be one of the all-time, ideal Christian marriages blew sky high, I was devastated for weeks. Part of my anguish was for the children who were being emotionally torn to shreds. But another part of me was saying, "How come I'm the last to know? Why didn't I see the warning signs with clarity instead of in hindsight? If divorce and infidelity could happen to them, could it happen to my marriage?"

A mutual acquaintance tells me, "My husband and I had some very heated discussions about that divorce. I took one side; he took the other. We finally decided we would never really know what happened."

Some people aren't willing to leave it at that; they will push for answers with their judgmental accusations: "Surely you don't think your son learned his irresponsibility on his own. I mean, everyone knows children model what they see at home."

If you admit to guilt when you aren't really guilty, the accuser will have an easy answer as to what happened. Go slowly with these people. If the person is your friend, a word of explanation may help the person. But chances are what happened is none of the person's business anyway.

The church. As Christians we are called to love our fellow man and demonstrate that love by our actions. All too often, we're all talk and little follow-through. Because we have never experienced certain situations or are unwilling to face them, we opt for pat answers that drive people away from the church instead of closer to it.

"Church was one of the worst things that happened to me," says Rosalita, speaking frankly. "I went to a Catholic school for awhile, a Christian school, a Baptist church on occasion, and I lived for periods of time with a Jewish lady. I've been exposed to a lot of religion.

"But I heard things like 'Jesus loves the little children.' No way. As a child, I would look in the mirror and tell myself I must be a miniature adult because Jesus *loves* little children. He couldn't possibly love me or He wouldn't let these bad things happen to me.

"Or I'd hear a Sunday School teacher say, 'You'd better be good because if you aren't you'll go to hell.' When you're already living in hell, it's hard to imagine anything worse.

"Once I attended a Vacation Bible school as a teenager and the young minister said, 'I'm here for you.' He wanted to be of help if anybody needed him. I desperately needed to tell someone about the abuse I had experienced, so I wrote him a note and asked to talk to him. Do you know what he did? He wrote a letter to my father asking my father to come with me. The minister never did talk directly to me. My father laid it on me about the letter and that was the end of that." Rosalita shakes her head, saying, "So often people's words are said without feeling."

People who live on the raw edge of life desperately need someone to listen to them — someone who will allow them to unburden their hearts without passing judgment. Whether we are at fault is not the issue in the beginning. What we need is a loving, caring environment with people who will keep our secrets and help us find release from the burden of guilt.

Fortunately, not everyone has the negative experience Rosalita had. For many people, the church provides the support and the love they need to get through difficult situations.

When Ingrid discovered that both of her children had been molested at the nursery school they attended, she was shocked, horrified and overwhelmed with guilt. Ingrid has found great help and hope by attending a support group at her church for parents whose children were molested or who themselves were molested as children.

CORRECTLY INTERPRETING SCRIPTURE

One of the passages of Scripture we often interpret incorrectly is found in 1 Timothy 3. Instead of using it to help hurting people, we hit them over the head with it, thus heaping a greater load of guilt on already desperate people.

In this passage Paul instructs a young pastor on how to select church leaders.

> Trustworthy is the saying, "Whoever aspires to the office of bishop desires to do a splendid work." The bishop, then, must be above reproach, the husband of only one wife, temperate, discreet . . . presiding well over his own home, keeping his children under control with complete respect, for if a person does not know enough to manage his own home, how will he take care of God's church? . . . A deacon should be the husband of one wife only, managing his children and his own household well (1 Timothy 3:1,2,5,6,12, Berkeley).

When Paul wrote these words to Timothy, he may have been thinking of the temptation of ministers and other Christian workers to spend more time at the church than with their own families. (This problem is certainly not limited to Christian workers.)

These verses encourage a person to establish the right priorities: family before church (or work). A parent who spends more time ministering to other people than to his own family will soon have no family at all. The family members may be present in the home, but the emotional distance between them will be enormous. Have you heard grown children of ministers or missionaries sorrowfully reflect, "My father was never home when I was growing up." Some children take out these frustrations by getting into trouble.

In the first chapter I told of a pastor and his wife whose children were unruly and often in trouble. The prolonged nature of the difficulties in this family were a good indication that this pastor needed to follow Paul's admonition and get out of the ministry until he could correct his faulty parenting skills. At the root of the problem were deep emotional problems that had never been resolved.

On the other hand, there is Ted — the pastor I mentioned at the beginning of this chapter — who overreacted to Paul's admonition. He and his wife had raised their children the best they knew how. What Ted failed to realize was that once his son became an adult, he was no longer responsible for his son's actions. Society does not hold him legally responsible — and neither does God. Remember the passage in Ezekiel 18 we discussed in chapter 5? Reread it if you've forgotten God's words of comfort.

I think we need to interpret the passage in 1 Timothy as God intended — lovingly. If every parent whose child did something wrong were forbidden to perform any church service, our churches would be empty! Isolated wrong-doing by a child does not a guilty parent make. But an overall pattern of immature or damaging parenting warrants adherence to the scriptural admonition. Before we can help someone else, we need to get the log out of our own eye.

HOW TO ANSWER YOUR ACCUSERS

What can you say when people criticize you? Is there a Christian way to counter the attacks of others? Listed below are seven typical accusations. In the space provided, write how you would answer the person's criticism.

Accusation
I didn't know your son was on drugs. How come you never told me?
What I Would Say

_____

_____.

Accusation
You and your wife are such nice people. I can't believe your daughter is actually an alcoholic.
What I Would Say

_____

_____.

Accusation
I understand your child is a real terror at school. Don't you ever discipline him?
What I Would Say

_____

_____.

Accusation
Your child is in trouble with the law and *you're* teaching Sunday School?
What I Would Say

_____

_____.

Accusation
I understand your married son is having an affair with another woman. Don't you think you should talk to him

and tell him what he's doing wrong? After all, you *are* his parent.
What I Would Say

_____

_____ .

Accusation
Well, your son may be in jail, but at least you have your other children at home. I hope nothing goes wrong with them.
What I Would Say

_____

_____ .

Accusation
I'm sorry to hear your son wandered off on your picnic and was so badly injured. You have to watch kids every minute.
What I Would Say

_____

_____ .

Now compare your answers with the suggested answers below. Sometimes the accusations are so absurd you may feel like giving an absurd answer! Other times a soft answer may cause the person to rethink his or her thoughtless comment.

The "What They Should Have Said" responses suggest what you might say when you're tempted to put the blame on someone without knowing all the facts.

They Say . . .
I didn't know you son was on drugs. How come you never told me?
But You Can Say . . .
It's not easy to talk about some things. Perhaps we can discuss it at another time.
What They Should Have Said . . .
This must be a scary time for you. Let's have lunch together next week.

They Say . . .
You and your wife are such nice people. I can't believe your daughter is actually an alcoholic.
But You Can Say . . .
Some things are hard to accept, aren't they?
What They Should Have Said . . .
I'm so sorry to hear about your daughter. How is she responding to the treatment?

They Say . . .
I understand your child is a real terror at school. Don't you ever discipline him?
But You Can Say . . .
No, never. We're trying very hard to raise a hellion!
What They Should Have Said . . .
Nothing!

They Say . . .
Your child is in trouble with the law and *you're* teaching Sunday School?
But You Can Say . . .
I'm sorry if that offends you. Perhaps we should talk about how you feel.
What They Should Have Said . . .
(Instead of hitting a distraught parent with both barrels, talk to your pastor and find out what your church's policy is on such matters.)

They Say . . .
I understand your married son is having an affair with another woman. Don't you think you should talk to him and tell him what he's doing is wrong? After all, you *are* his parent.
But You Can Say . . .
What our son is doing is very upsetting to us. However, he is a grown man and must live with the consequences of his own decisions.
What They Should Have Said . . .
It must be very difficult to keep still and not try to run your son's life for him. I admire your courage.

They Say . . .
Well, your son may be in jail, but at least you have your other children at home. I hope nothing goes wrong with them.
But You Can Say . . .
So do we.
What They Should Have Said . . .
You must feel very lonely with your son gone. Could I bring dinner over some afternoon when you go to visit him?

They Say . . .
I'm sorry to hear your son wandered off on your picnic and was so badly injured. You have to watch kids every minute.
But You Can Say . . .
Thank you for caring.
What They Should Have Said . . .
That must have been a terrifying experience for both you and your son. I've been praying that his leg would heal properly.

The psalmist David certainly had his share of accusers. But his best defense was to ask God to deal with them. He laments in these words:

> O LORD, fight those fighting me; declare war on them for their attacks on me . . . For though I did them no wrong, yet they laid a trap for me and dug a pitfall in my path . . . These evil men swear to a lie. They accuse me of things I have never even heard about . . . Rise up, O LORD my God; vindicate me. Declare me "not guilty," for you are just (Psalm 35:1,7,11,23,24 TLB).

9

LEARNING TO LET GO OF YOUR CHILDREN

Smothering a child by anxious concern over every detail of his life, robbing him of all opportunities to express himself naturally and to discover the world for himself, rebuking his early efforts to explore and direct his dawning sexuality, may be more crippling than beatings and curses.

Dr. Carl Menninger
A Psychiatrist's World

Jeff was the father of two boys by the time his marriage broke up. His wife split, leaving him with the little ones. Jeff and the boys moved back home with his mom and dad.

What's so unusual about that? Nothing. The same thing happens all the time. We can understand a divorced father's need for security in the early stages after a divorce. It's difficult for a working father to care for young children without some help.

But there's more to the story. In Jeff's case, moving home was the symptom of a greater problem and possibly a contributing factor to his divorce as well. After several years, Jeff and the boys are still living at home because Mom and Dad have taken over and made life easy for Jeff. They provide a roof over his head and they take care of his children. He does practically nothing to help around his parents' home. Seldom, if ever, does he make an effort to do things with his boys. Once he and his girlfriend got an apartment, but in a couple of months Jeff and the boys were right back at Mom and Dad's.

Bob and Lila, Jeff's parents, are helping their son remain a child.

One of the most important lessons we as parents must learn is to let go of our adult children and to let them live with the consequences of their decisions. That is easy to do if they are making right choices. It is not so easy to do if they are making wrong ones, but it's the only way they will ever grow up.

How do we hold on to our children?

One of the ways we do it is by *covering for them*. If Tim regularly stays out late at a party and is too tired to go to school or work the next day, we call and say he is not feeling well. If Shelley is rude and obnoxious to our guests, we say she is not really like that — she's just going through a phase. If our kids get in any kind of a jam, they know dear old Mom and Dad will always be there to bail them out.

Another way we hold on to our children is by *thinking we can play God*. I call this the power play. These are well-meaning but often strong-willed parents who think they can right the wrongs in their kids' lives.

Did Todd smash up his sports car? That's OK — Dad will buy him a new one.

Did Melissa get herself pregnant? Then Mom will raise the child herself, or force Melissa to put the baby up for adoption or, worse yet, encourage her to get an abortion. Mom will solve the problem, not Melissa.

Did Eric barely make it through college because he was too busy partying and having a good time? That's OK. Dad will use his influence to get him a good-paying job, regardless of his low academic record.

Is twenty-nine-year-old David still living at home? With no encouragement from his parents to move out, why should he? Mom does his laundry and picks up after him. Dad keeps his car in good repair. A hot meal is always ready when he comes home from work. He doesn't have to pay rent on one of those apartments that requires first and last month's rent and a cleaning deposit. He's able to save a bundle by living at home and he's able to spend a bundle — on a new sports car, a boat, good clothes. Mom and Dad like his company and David's got it made. But David is not learning how to deal with the real world — the world of cleaning deposits, utility bills, keeping house and doing laundry.

In short, David is ripping off his parents — and they're loving it. Why? Because they are still in control!

WHY WE HOLD ON

In his book *Cutting Loose,* author Howard M. Halpern advises children:

> In every parent there is a wish that his or her children grow up to be strong, independent, effective people. And in every parent there is a wish that his or her children remain weak, dependent, ineffectual people . . . the parent's desire to see his offspring grow and be independent comes from the mature parenting part of himself, while *the parent's desire to have his offspring remain attached and dependent comes from the little child within the parent.*[1]

Why do parents hold on to their children through thick and thin? Often the root of the problem can be traced to one or both parents who have never developed their own lives apart from their children. Most often it is the mother who finds herself in this position. For most of her married life she has put all energies into rearing her children. She never stopped to ask, "What will my life be like after the children are gone? What are my personal goals? What do I want to accomplish in this world apart from my children? What kind of goals should my husband and I be setting for our life together without children?"

When her children reach the age when they should be leading their own lives, she is highly threatened by the idea of letting go. After all, she has no life apart from them.

Admittedly, it's hard to let go even when we know we must.

"I was not prepared for the shock when my oldest child announced she wanted to move out and get her own apartment," says Ruth. "I had done all the right things. I had gone back to school to finish my education. I had a new career to look forward to and new interests. But I still wasn't prepared for what her leaving did to me."

Sometimes parents hold on to their children because they desperately need to be needed. They may actually thrive on the turmoil caused by their errant children. As long as the children are having trouble and turning to Mom and Dad for help the parents feel needed.

LEARNING TO LET GO

How can we learn to let go of our children? Sometimes it's easier said than done. But it is a process that must begin almost as soon as they are born. In the marriage relationship, we seek ways to tie ourselves more closely to our mate. In parenting, we must build a relationship that will eventually separate the children from us. This is not abandonment. This is maturity.

One of the hardest things we must learn is when to *stop* being a protective parent. Our job is not to be the eternal mother and father to whom Johnny can run whenever life gets tough. If our children are to grow and mature, we must gradually turn every aspect of their lives over to them. We cannot wipe their noses and type their term papers forever.

In *Parents in Pain*, author John White discusses the need to let go of many of the ideals we have regarding parenthood, especially when our children make wrong choices. This includes relinquishing our right to be proud of our children and the right to uninterrupted enjoyment of them. It means giving up our right to possess our children and being willing to forego any repayment for what we have done for them. Relinquishment means giving up our right to uninterrupted tranquility with our children and our right to respectability. It also means allowing our children to face pain and tragedy and to let them accept the consequences of their behavior.[2]

These are not easy things to give up, but as White points out,

> It follows that if God's greatest desires for his creatures have not always been fulfilled, our desires for our children may not always be fulfilled either. It is better that we aim at being godly parents even though we may fail to produce perfect children, than that we aim at being social scientists employing techniques which, were they successful, would change the parent/child relationship to a technician/object relationship.[3]

OUR CHILDREN ARE UNIQUE

One of the most important aspects of letting go is realizing that our children are unique individuals created by God. They are not an extension of ourselves. God has not given us absolute control over our children's every action. Therefore, He does not hold us accountable for everything they do wrong. Nor, on the other hand, can we take credit for everything they do right! As Margie and Greg Lewis write:

> As we allow a child a growing independence, we have also to wean ourselves from accountability. I've talked to some parents who refuse to do this. Their young adult children are independent in every other way, but the mother and father still blame themselves for any sins the children commit. We need to realize some things are beyond our control. In many cases, it's not that the parenting was lacking or weak, but the world's temptations and attractions are so strong. The failure to realize this produces unnecessary guilt.[4]

GIVE GOD FREEDOM TO WORK

A second way we can begin to let go is by giving God the freedom to work in our children's lives as He sees fit — according to His time schedule, not ours. It is our nature to hope and pray for miracles. But sometimes, because of our stubborn wills, we (as well as our children) learn best from our mistakes.

Remember the story of the prodigal son in Luke 15? Two boys raised in the same environment. The younger brother decides to split and take with him the Mercedes, the gold stock and his dad's charge cards. The older brother adjusts his halo and says he wouldn't *think* of doing such a thing.

The rebellious son *leaves* home.

The "model" son *stays* home.

Nowhere do you read that the father wallowed in introspection and self-pity, wondering what he had done wrong as a parent. Despite the shame his younger son was bringing upon the family, the father refused to give in to constant self-recrimination.

When his son finally comes home, penniless and repentant, does the father lay him out for running away from home, totalling the car, wasting his money and disgracing the family name? I probably would. But no, he *throws a party* to celebrate his son's return!

A party? Come now! How about grounding him for a month? Or making him work to pay back all the money he blew on drugs and booze and women?

No, he throws a party to celebrate the return of his beloved son. You see, that father was able to do what is often difficult for parents to do. He was able to look past his own mistakes and the bad behavior of his son to the *person* of his son. In this case, he saw that his son was truly repentant.

Looking past the behavior to the person is not easy to do. But isn't that what God does with us? If He were to accept us on the basis of our good behavior, none of us would make it. Rather, He looks past our sin and failures, which He has already forgiven, to the person He knows we can become.

The prodigal son learned from his bad choices and grew because of them. Maybe God knew that making some bad choices was the only way he would learn some valuable lessons. The older son who stayed home and kept his nose clean didn't learn a thing. He was jealous and angry when his errant brother was given a party in his honor and he was not.

No doubt that father longed many times for his younger son's return — wondered where he was, if he was safe, why he didn't write or at least call home collect. But God's timing was not the father's timing. And it is obvious that that father grew spiritually through the tragic circumstances of his son's life.

When our children go wrong we are angry and hurt. The last thing we would think of doing is throwing a party. Doesn't that just condone what that "stupid kid" has done?

Yet that's exactly what God does for us. He's throwing a giant party for us. It's called eternal life. We enter through the doorway of forgiveness from all our sins. (Every evil thing that son had done was left outside the door of his father's house when he finally returned home).

But growth and healing take time — in our lives and in the lives of our children. Sometimes God interjects a miracle. But more often than not, He works through circumstances and other people to help both our children and us to grow and mature.

"The healing process is not always what we think it should be," write Dave and Jan Stoop who had struggled for years with a wayward son. They continue:

> There is something much deeper going on, that we sometimes catch a glimpse of, that transcends our need for an immediate solution to a pressing problem. It's so easy to get caught up in a system, even a system of faith, that guarantees specific results. In our efforts to put into practice the principles of trusting, committing and resting, we found ourselves stepping into the area of presumption because we lost sight of who was in charge . . .
>
> We desperately struggled with our "system" of faith.

> Sitting at coffee with a friend one day, at the darkest point of our struggle, he pressed us for an answer to the question of where God's sovereignty fit into our "system." In our search for a miracle, we lost sight of the object of our faith — God, Himself. As we reaffirmed our trust in His sovereignty, we discovered the miracle was already taking place. The miracle was taking place — *within us!*[5]

THE VALUE OF A CREATIVE CRISIS

A third way we can learn to let go is by understanding the value of a creative crisis. For most of us, including our children, change often does not take place without some kind of a crisis.

A wife spends years covering for her husband's sometimes erratic behavior caused by his drinking. She makes excuses for him, takes over chores he was supposed to do and tries to make people see the good in him. And the result is that he keeps on drinking. No change takes place.

Then one day she realizes she cannot go on living with an alcoholic husband. She tells him to pack his bags and not to come home until he has been sober for six months. Suddenly the husband is confronted with the reality of his sickness and the need to make a drastic change in the way he lives. If his family means anything to him at all, in all likelihood he will seek help.

In his excellent book, *How to Have a Creative Crisis*, Norm Wright says:

> Many crisis situations which we experience would not have to occur if we took charge of the situation early on and created a positive, controlled crisis ourselves! Does that sound shocking, unchristian, radical? It may at first, but look again at two key words: *positive* and *controlled*. A positive, controlled crisis can be the catalyst to change an intolerable situation.[6]

How do we create a positive and controlled crisis in

our errant children's lives? Sometimes, as in the case of minors, direct intervention by the parents is needed. But sometimes we can create just such a crisis by letting go and allowing the child to face the reality of what he or she is doing.

If you stop loaning the rent money every other month to your son who can't hold a job, he will be forced to face the fact that something is wrong with his attitude toward work. If you require him to pay back what he's borrowed, you will be helping him face adult responsibility.

If you stop running a free babysitting center for your grandchildren, your children will be forced to find a good day care facility so Grandma has some time to call her own. Or one parent will have to quit work until the children are school age.

Letting go means telling your son that the next time he runs out of gasoline he will walk home. You will no longer pick him up in the middle of the night.

A positive and controlled crisis simply means the child is finally forced to live with the consequences of his or her decisions. No more will Mummy and Daddy be around to take care of things.

The psalmist confirms the value of a creative crisis when he says:

> Before I was afflicted, I went astray; but now I keep thy saying . . . It is good for me that I was afflicted, so that I may learn Thy statutes (Psalm 119:67,71, Berkeley).

PRAYING FOR OUR CHILDREN

Part of being both a friend and a parent to our children is praying for them. But our prayers must be according to God's will, not our own. Will God answer our prayers that Sue follow a certain profession of *our* choice, or that Bob will marry the girl of *our* choice? Sounds absurd, doesn't it? But how often do we pray just that way?

Then what should we pray for that is in line with

God's will? Pray that they will put their faith and trust in God and follow His leading in their lives. *That* is His will. Such a prayer is easy to pray when our children *are* following the Lord. But suppose they are not.

As parents we often look to Proverbs 22:6 for comfort:

> Train up a child in the way he should go and when he is old, he will not depart from it (KJV).

This verse can give us hope, or it can bring us to despair — even doubting God and His Word.

"If my child is supposed to return to the Lord," you ask, "why hasn't he?"

It all depends on how we interpret that verse.

I think we need to begin by realizing that when the writer of Proverbs made that statement, he was saying that this is normally the case, because a proverb describes normal results of human behavior. But God also makes it clear in His Word that each child is responsible for his or her own decisions. There will be times when our children don't live up to our training or expectations.

What the writer is saying in Proverbs 22:6 is, "If you give a child instruction in a particular way of life (this could be vocational, along the lines of the child's natural abilities, as well as spiritual), in all likelihood the child will follow that path." But not always, and not always according to our timetable.

If we have faithfully reared our children in the faith, and if they have genuinely accepted Christ as Lord and Savior of their lives, they will probably follow that course for life. And if they do stray away, they may come back "when they are old." But when is old? Is it age twenty? Or forty-five? Or ninety? Only God knows their hearts. In the meantime we can thank and praise God for what He is going to do and is doing in their lives.

LEADING A CHILD TO INDEPENDENCE

When their children were young, Paul and Jeannie

McKean became very concerned about their children's future. They decided to lay some definite plans that would help their children become responsible, independent adults. Jeannie writes:

> . . . my mind began to wander to some disturbing things I had been reading in the newspapers, of teenage runaways and rebellion, of middle-class kids facing drug arrests, and of the lack of a sense of morality in general. Looking around the Christian community, I received little assurance that our children would be immune. As I tried to picture what they would be like at age eighteen, I became aware of a sense of panic. How could I know that someday I wouldn't see Todd or Tanya's picture in the paper and experience heartache for them as well as myself? How could I prepare these precious children for the years to come? How could I lead them to the independence that arises from a solid dependence on God?[7]

Out of this deep concern for their children's future, Paul and Jeannie developed a tangible plan of action to lead their children to independence — spiritually, physically, intellectually, socially, emotionally and financially. In their book, *Leading a Child to Independence* (Here's Life Publishers), they outline a very workable plan that you can adapt and use with your own children.

When their children reached the mid-point of their senior year in high school, Paul and Jeannie presented each child with a "Declaration of Independence" certificate and special gift to mark their "graduation" into adulthood. I highly recommend this book for its positive and practical suggestions.

FROM PARENT TO FRIEND

In her excellent book, *Once My Child . . . Now My Friend,* Elinor Lenz offers practical suggestions on how to shift gears from being a parent to your children to being their friend. While admittedly this is not easy, this transition is vital to establishing an adult-to-adult relationship with your grown children.

In order to disconnect yourself from the parenting role, she suggests:

- Don't offer unsolicited advice or assistance. Assume that your children can solve their own problems and that if they can't, you probably can't do it for them.
- Avoid any suggestion of a mother/father-knows-best stance. A posture of superior wisdom is fatal to any honest exchange of views between adults.
- Don't try to manipulate the course of events in your adult children's lives . . .
- Resist the temptation to protect your adult children from "the slings and arrows of outrageous fortune." Once they are grown there is no way you can shield them from the hurts and pangs and disappointments of adult life. You can offer sympathy and understanding as you would to a contemporary, but that's about it . . .
- Never, under any circumstances, make your son or daughter feel guilty for not phoning or visiting you as often as you'd like. A sense of obligation is a pathetic substitute for a genuine desire to make contact . . .
- Eliminate from your consciousness any traces of self-pity or martyrdom. "After all I've done for you — " are words that should never cross your lips . . .
- Bite your tongue whenever you are tempted to make comparisons with the way it was when you were your children's age . . .[8]

She goes on to point out that learning new responses toward our children does not mean that our love is any different for them.

> What happens is that we learn to love them in a new way, not because they are ours, but because they are *they*. In reconnecting, we liberate each other from the molds that have been compressing our human selves; we are then free to come together as good friends who share a common set of memories.[9]

Think for a moment about your own closest personal friend. What is he or she like? Chances are this person:

. . . listens with empathy when you have a problem,

but does not make judgmental statements about what you are going through.

. . . does not try to solve your problem for you.

. . . keeps confidences, but does not try to make you feel guilty if you do not feel like confiding.

. . . does not attach strings to your relationship but rather leaves you free to be yourself.

That, dear parents, is the kind of friend your grown children want you to be to them.

10

LEARNING TO LET GO OF GUILT

Jesus said to them, "You are truly my disciples if you live as I tell you to, and you will know the truth, and the truth will set you free."
John 8:32, TLB

Cindy had always been a mouthy kid, saying exactly how she felt about things. But overall she hadn't given her parents, Don and Laura, any real problems.

Then in seventh grade, everything changed. Sweet Cindy became rebellious Cindy. Her father was in the hospital with a life-threatening illness. With Laura spending much of her time at the hospital, Cindy took advantage of the extra freedom available to her.

In the last three years she has run away seven or eight times, ditched school repeatedly and finally quit altogether. She takes drugs. Cindy seems hellbent on destroying her own life and making life for her parents as miserable as possible. She manipulates them and refuses to do anything they ask her to do.

"I want to be a strict parent," says Don, discouraged, "but I also want to be a fair parent." Yet any restrictions placed on her, no matter how fair, are unfair in Cindy's eyes.

Cindy is the boss.

It's not that her parents haven't tried. In fact, they've tried everything to bring their daughter under control and to help her straighten out her life. They have gone for counseling. They have wept, prayed and pledged their undying love to Cindy and they have also told her to leave the house and never come back.

"I've gone to the school — gone everywhere — for help," says Laura, "but the only real help I've found has been from the church. In my desperation I once took Cindy to the police station and told them to take her because I couldn't do a thing with her. But, of course, they wouldn't take her because she hadn't broken a law. They told me there was no way I could leave her with them."

"I have hoped she would really break a law," admits Don, "so she would finally have to pay for her actions."

And Laura confesses, "I have even hoped she would break a leg or two so that *something* would slow her down and stop her from running with the wrong kids and getting into trouble."

Cindy is not about to be grounded by anybody. She knows that running away is not a punishable crime, so she even gets away with that.

"The only crime," says Laura, "is if *we* refuse to take responsibility for her when the police find her."

Don's voice was barely controlled when he told me, "We have asked ourselves over and over again what we did wrong to make her this way. I even asked her one time what on earth I could possibly have done to make her so rebellious. She told me I had done nothing wrong. 'Then why are you acting like this?' I asked. Cindy had no answer."

"I've been afraid to turn her out of the house completely," Laura continues, "because I keep thinking that a fifteen-year-old girl will end up as a prostitute or a drug addict. She has no skills and she can't get a job anyway unless she is in school and has a work permit."

"I really don't believe it's my fault she's like this," Don

says. "She made a commitment to Christ when she was younger and she's grown up in a Christian home. I have to believe things are going to turn out all right for Cindy someday. *I have to believe that."*

How do you let go of a rebellious child like Cindy who doesn't seem to suffer the consequences of her misbehavior? Obviously, you cannot totally let go of a minor child when the law holds you personally responsible for her.

But you can learn to let go of the guilt.

In the preceding chapters we have discussed some factors that affect the decisions a child will make about his or her thoughts and actions. We have noted the areas over which we parents must take responsibility and the factors over which we have no control. We have discussed God's precise expectations of us as parents, and what He doesn't expect from us.

"I understand all that intellectually," you may be saying, "but inside I still feel guilty."

"All of us look back over our years of parenthood and find real, justified reasons for our guilt," writes Margie M. Lewis in *The Hurting Parent.* "But I have discovered that much, if not most, of the guilt which plagues hurting mothers and fathers is unnecessary, false guilt."[1]

Here are some principles to help you rid yourself of false guilt and accept forgiveness for any real sins you may have committed.

TRUE GUILT VERSUS FALSE GUILT

Learn to differentiate between true and false guilt. The first thing we must do when our children make wrong choices is to think logically. Yet that is often the last thing we do. John White writes:

> I have a feeling . . . that when doubts and anxieties assail us, common sense is the first thing to go. We long for easy answers, unambiguous assurance. The doubts and guilts drown our minds and make us not *want* to

think rationally but instead to cling to any bit of ideological driftwood that comes along. The last thing we want to do when we are drowning is to think logically.

Yet think we must.[2]

Instead of thinking logically about what has happened and determining whether someone is actually to blame, we think emotionally. Our emotions are easily betrayed. We end up allowing Satan to trap us into feeling guilty for something that in actuality we have not done wrong. Bruce Narramore and Bill Counts assure parents:

> The first question we should ask ourselves when we feel a tinge of guilt is, *"Did I really blow it?"* In other words, we want to determine if we really did something wrong or if we only violated the childish standards of our ideal self — our inner parent. Most of us feel guilty over a number of things God doesn't consider sin.[3]

True guilt is the result of breaking one of God's laws. False guilt results from failing to live up to our own unrealistic ideal of what we think a parent should be. False guilt is a powerful tool of the devil, according to James Dobson:

> Second Corinthians 11:14 indicates that Satan presents himself as "an angel of light," meaning he speaks as a false representative of God. Accordingly, it has been my observation that undeserved guilt is one of the most powerful weapons in the devil's arsenal. By seeming to ally himself with the voice of the Holy Spirit, Satan uses the conscience to accuse, torment and berate his victims. What better tool for spiritual discouragement could there be than feelings of guilt which cannot be "forgiven" — because they do not represent genuine disapproval from God?[4]

RE-EDUCATE YOUR CONSCIENCE

If false guilt is a recurring problem, then it's time to start re-educating your conscience. The conscience was created by God and is often used by the Holy Spirit to show us when we have done wrong. But just as our bodies must be programmed with the right foods, rest, and exercise in order to be healthy and perform well, so our conscience must be "programmed" with the right material if it is to be an accurate indicator of guilt.

The Bible talks about a "pure conscience" (1 Timothy 3:9), a "good conscience" (Acts 23:1), and a "conscience bearing witness" (Romans 2:15). It also talks about a "weak conscience" (1 Corinthians 8:7), a "defiled conscience" (Titus 1:15), and a "conscience seared with a hot iron" (1 Timothy 4:2). Narramore and Counts state it this way:

> If our conscience is over-educated and we feel guilty about things the Bible doesn't say are sin, we must learn to reject those extra-biblical standards and focus only on God's expectations for us . . . We must learn that the guilt motivations of the punitive self never come from God. We must learn to realize these accusations are stimulated by the devil.[5]

Look at these comforting words found in 1 John 3:18-23 (NIV):

> Dear children, let us not love with words or tongue but with actions and in truth. This then is how we know that we belong to the truth, and how we set our hearts at rest in his presence whenever our hearts condemn us. For God is greater than our hearts, and he knows everything.
> Dear friends, if our hearts do not condemn us, we have confidence before God and receive from him anything we ask, because we obey his commands and do what pleases him. And this is his command: to believe in the name of his Son, Jesus Christ, and to love one another as he commanded us.

The material to be programmed into our conscience and into our lives is found in the pages of Scripture, beginning with the verses you have just read. For *as a man thinks in his heart, so is he.*

DO NOT WALLOW IN REGRET

Do not wallow in regret, remorse or disappointment which only serve to keep your guilt alive. It is perfectly natural even after we have confessed wrong and received forgiveness, to deeply regret wrongs which we have committed. It is also natural to feel profound disappointment and hurt when our children make wrong choices. But we must not dwell on the past. Only when we are willing to lay our hurts and our unfulfilled dreams at the foot of the cross will we be able to grow and mature.

I have mentioned in an earlier book that our first child was stillborn. After nine months of joyful anticipation, our dreams and hopes met with harsh reality. Our little boy was dead and nothing could undo that fact.

We mourned our loss as any parents would do. For six weeks after his birth (and death) I cried every night when I went to bed. But eventually the tears stopped. They had to, if life for my husband and me was to move forward.

Prolonging one's grief is unhealthy and non-productive. It does not bring back the person who has died. But it creates for the grieving parent a "living death." Prolonging our grief over a dead child means we have not really accepted death. By the same token, to continually berate ourselves for real or imagined failures means we have not really accepted forgiveness.

God's forgiveness also brings His healing. If we will let Him, He can heal our memories as surely as He can heal our bodies.

FIND POSITIVE FRIENDS

Cultivate friendships with Christians who will encourage you in your acceptance of God's forgiveness, not heap a greater guilt upon you. The less we are able to accept imperfection in ourselves, the more critical we tend to be of others. Some people seem to major on that theme. We should limit our contacts with such people and seek out those who can build us up.

Bruce Narramore and Bill Counts tell of a woman in a group counseling session who had felt guilty over a past sin for many years and was unable to accept God's forgiveness. After she had haltingly confessed her secret sin of the past, her husband put his arms around her and said, "Honey, I forgive you." Through that simple but genuine act she was finally able to feel God's forgiveness.

> In like ways, each of us represents God to one another. This is one reason the Bible stresses the importance of close relationships with other Christians. We are to become a source of each other's new ideals. And as we are lovingly forgiven and corrected we begin to see how God might do the same. When we "confess our faults to each other and pray for each other" we gain a deeper sense of the reality of God's love and forgiveness.[6]

ACCEPT UNCONDITIONAL FORGIVENESS

Recognize that true forgiveness is an all-encompassing act. If we cannot forgive other people (including our children) for what they do wrong, then in all likelihood we won't be able to forgive ourselves for real or imagined wrongs — and vice versa. Nor will we be able to truly accept the forgiveness that Christ offers to us.

Remember the part of the Lord's Prayer that says, "Forgive us our debts as we forgive others"? Why did God put a condition on our forgiveness? Because He knows that one without the other is not really forgiveness. It has to be an all-encompassing cycle to be complete: God forgives me, I forgive myself, I also forgive others. The cycle is complete whether the other person who has wronged me asks for my forgiveness or not. Because of God's forgiveness, I can forgive the other person and I can also forgive myself.

"But," you say, "my child, the apple of my eye, has

wronged me terribly. He has brought shame on the family and shipwreck to his own life. How on earth can I forgive?"

You can't. But God working through you *can.* "It is God who works in you, inspiring both the will and the deed, for his own chosen purpose" (Philippians 2:13, NEB).

WORK ON YOUR SELF-ESTEEM

Be aware of the close tie between recurring feelings of guilt and low self-esteem. The person who always feels the need to take the blame is usually the person who sees himself as a person of little worth. It is no surprise, then, that such a person automatically takes the blame when his or her children make wrong choices. This person constantly looks within to find the cause of things that go wrong.

"Surprisingly," says Earl Jabay in his book, *Search for Identity,* "there is very little Scripture which urges us to look within. The biblical thrust seems to be two-fold: (1) that *God* rather than man is the searcher of human hearts (1 Chronicles 28:9; Psalms 26:2, 139:1,23; Jeremiah 17:10; 1 Corinthians 2:10); (2) that though we are to look within, it is more important to look *up* to God in faith (Proverbs 3:5; Hebrews 12:2).[7]

If we are living with guilt on a daily basis, it is a clear indication that something else is wrong.

There are many books on the market on the subject of self-esteem. If you are living with guilt that will not go away, I urge you to read on the subject of self-esteem and/or seek professional Christian counseling. God never intended for you to live with a steady diet of guilt. In fact, He sent His Son to earth for the express purpose of setting you *free* from guilt. Why not accept His pardon and allow Him to set you free?

WE ARE ALL AMATEURS

Do you know any people who are professional parents? Having completed X-number of years of schooling in the profession of parenting, they have certified degrees and are able to handle any and all parenting problems with ease and grace. They are never upset over uncertainties, never out of control, totally unflappable. They are pros.

I've yet to meet any. And I never expect to become one. Quite frankly, I'm an amateur at parenting — and so are you. You may have completed the Red Cross course on how to change a baby doll with flying colors. But the first time that *real* doll of yours, who is all kicks and squirms, sticks her feet in her dirty diaper, you do not feel very professional.

You may read and memorize a dozen ways to discipline a child, but when none of them works on *your* child, you throw away the books and start over.

Just when you've figured out how to handle the first child, along comes number two — and three, and four — who are totally different from number one and require a whole new set of guidelines.

THE TRUTH CAN SET YOU FREE

Appropriate for yourself the fact that Christ came to free us from the burden of guilt, not heap a greater burden upon us.

In the synagogue, Jesus read from the book of Isaiah regarding the whole purpose of His coming to earth:

> The Spirit of the Lord is on me,
>   because he has anointed me
>   to preach good news to the poor.
> He has sent me to proclaim freedom
>   for the prisoners
>   and recovery of sight for the blind,
> to release the oppressed,
>   to proclaim the year of the Lord's

favor.
                    Luke 4:18, Isaiah 61:1,2, NIV).

Jesus also said, "You are truly my disciples if you live as I tell you to, and you will know the truth, and the truth will set you free" (John 8:32, TLB).

The truth about what?

The truth about yourself as a parent — your strengths and your weaknesses, your abilities and your limitations.

The truth about your children as individuals — their God-given uniqueness, their individuality.

The truth about God's power to save and to forgive — and to help you forgive yourself.

Jesus said, "I have come that they may have life, and have it to the full (John 10:10b, NIV)."

Parents who are living life to the full are not weighed down with a load of guilt.

Notes

Chapter 1
1. *U.S. News & World Report,* March 7, 1983, "'Parent Burnout' Latest Sign of Today's Stresses," p. 76.
2. Dave and Jan Stoop, *A Parent's Cry for Help* (Harvest House, 1981), p. 65.
3. John White, *Parents in Pain* (Inter-Varsity Press, 1979), p. 22.

Chapter 2
1. Philippe Ariès, *Centuries of Childhood,* A Social History of Family Life, translated from the French by Robert Baldick (New York: Alfred A. Knopf, 1962), p. 411.
2. *Ibid.*, p. 43.
3. *Ibid.*, p. 43.
4. John Locke, *Some Thoughts Concerning Education,* abridged and edited by F. W. Garforth (Woodbury, NY: Barron's Educational Series, Inc., 1964), p. 64.
5. Robert I. Watson and Henry Clay Lindgren, *Psychology of the Child* (Third Edition), (New York: John Wiley and Sons, Inc., 1973), p. 5.
6. Ariès, *Op. Cit.*, p. 412.
7. Watson and Lindgren, *Op. Cit.*, p. 6
8. R. Murray Thomas, *Comparing Theories of Child Development* (Belmont, CA: Wadsworth Publishing Company, Inc., 1979), p. 434.
9. *Ibid.*, p. 32
10. Reprinted from the book *What Do I Do Wrong?: Mothers, Children and Guilt,* copyright ©1985 by Lynn Caine. Reprinted by permission of Arbor House Publishing Company. Pp. 12, 13.
11. *Ibid.*, p. 16.

Chapter 3
1. William V. Arnold, *The Power of Your Perceptions* (Philadelphia: The Westminster Press, 1984).

Chapter 5
1. Stanton E. Samenow, *Inside the Criminal Mind* (New York: Times Books, 1984), p. xiii.
2. *Ibid.,* pp. 25, 26.
3. Knofel Station, *Bible Keys for Today's Family* (Cincinnati: New Life Books, 1984), p. 111.
4. Stanton E. Samenow, *Op. Cit.,* pp. 45, 46.

Chapter 6
1. Harold H. Bloomfield, M.D. with Leonard Felder, Ph.D., *Making Peace with Your Parents* (New York: Random House, 1983), p. 207.
2. Samuel Osherson, *Finding our Fathers: The Unfinished Business of Manhood* (New York: The Free Press, 1986), pp. 10-11.
3. Harold H. Bloomfield, *Op. Cit.,* p. 41. For further amplification of these five steps, see pages 31-42.
4. Samuel Osherson, *Op. Cit.,* pp. 197-198.
5. Lewis B. Smedes, *Forgive and Forget: Healing the Hurts We Don't Deserve* (San Francisco: Harper & Row, 1984), p. 149.
6. *Ibid.,* p. 124.

Chapter 7
1. Cecil G. Osborn, *Self Esteem, Overcoming Inferiority Feelings* (Nashville: Abington Press, 1986), pp. 28-29.
2. Craig W. Ellison, Editor, *Your Better Self: Christianity, Psychology and Self-esteem* (San Francisco: Harper & Row, 1983), p. 23.
3. *Ibid.,* p. 30.
4. *Ibid.,* p. 34-35.
5. Janet Congo, *Finding Inner Security: A Woman's Quest for Interdependence* (Ventura, CA: Regal Books, 1985), pp. 50-51.
6. H. Norman Wright, *Making Peace With Your Past* (Old Tappan, N.J.: Fleming H. Revell Company, 1985), pp. 50-51.

Chapter 9
1. Howard M. Halpern, *Cutting Loose, An Adult Guide*

to *Coming to Terms With Your Parents* (New York: Bantam Books, 1976), p. 13.
2. John White, *Parents in Pain* (Downers Grove, Illinois: InterVarsity Press, 1979). See chapter 9.
3. *Ibid.*, p. 164.
4. Margie M. Lewis with Gregg Lewis, *The Hurting Parent* (Grand Rapids, Michigan: Zondervan, 1980)., p. 95.
5. Dave and Jan Stoop, *A Parent's Cry for Help* (Eugene, Oregon: Harvest House Publishers, 1981), pp. 127, 128.
6. H. Norman Wright, *How to Have a Creative Crisis* (Waco, Texas: Word Books, 1986), p. 107.
7. Paul and Jeannie McKean and Maggie Bruehl, *Leading a Child to Independence* (San Bernardino, CA: Here's Life Publishers, 1986), pp. 15, 16.
8. Elinor Lenz, *Once My Child . . . Now My Friend* (New York: Warner Books, 1981), pp. 61-63.
9. *Ibid.*, p. 64.

Chapter 10
1. Margie M. Lewis with Gregg Lewis, *The Hurting Parent* (Grand Rapids: Michigan: Zondervan, 1980), p. 94.
2. John White, *Parents in Pain* (Downers Grove, Illinois: InterVarsity Press, 1979), p. 28.
3. Bruce Narramore and Bill Counts, *Guilt and Freedom* (Santa Ana, California: Vision House Publishers, 1974), p. 119.
4. Dr. James Dobson, *Emotions: Can You Trust Them?* (Ventura, California: Regal Books, 1980), pp. 22,23.
5. Narramore and Counts, *Op. Cit.,* p. 154.
6. *Ibid.,* pp. 157,158.
7. Earl Jabay, *Search for Identity* (Grand Rapids, Michigan: Zondervan, 1967), p. 26.

More Help for Parents

BUILDING YOUR MATE'S SELF-ESTEEM
By Dennis & Barbara Rainey

The national bestseller — presents ten building blocks to help married couples enhance each other's self-image and confidence. The authors are directors of the country's fastest-growing family conference ministry.

951343/$7.95

LEADING A CHILD TO INDEPENDENCE
By Paul & Jeannie McKean and Maggie Bruehl

How to prepare your child for responsible adulthood . . . a positive approach to raising children through the teens.

Foreword by H. Norman Wright 951459/$7.95

INTIMATE MOMENTS
By Eva Gibson

A breakthrough approach to help parents guide their children into a personal walk with God. Includes creative Bible study ideas to do as a family.

951467/$5.95

Available at Christian bookstores everywhere.

Or order directly from HERE'S LIFE PUBLISHERS, P.O. Box 88054, Grand Rapids, MI 49518. Enclose full payment plus $1.50 shipping and handling. California residents add 6% sales tax. MasterCard and Visa accepted. ALLOW SIX WEEKS FOR PROCESSING AND DELIVERY.